The Light in the Library Basement

A Personal Finance Mystery Story

David Anderson

Camille Cabrera

The Light in the Library Basement
A Personal Finance Mystery Story

The Light in the Library Basement

A Personal Finance Mystery Story

A dark past haunts the Green Oaks Public Library, where strange happenings persist at the scene of a closed murder case. Sights and sounds in the basement drag an unsuspecting teenager into a hunt for clues. Eloise Alberty's life gets complicated when financial struggles, high school drama, and a new job collide with a possible murder. Eloise's dream purchase becomes a longshot as she juggles troubles in her small town. To navigate her minefield of challenges, Eloise must tap into her sleuthing skills and the personal finance insights of her family and friends – fast!

Disclaimer

This is a work of fiction. The information provided in this book is for entertainment purposes only and is not intended to constitute financial, legal, or tax advice. Investing and financial decisions involve risks and there is no guarantee of specific results. Readers should seek professional consultation for advice specific to their individual situation. By using this book, readers acknowledge and agree that they assume full responsibility for their financial decisions and understand that the content is not a substitute for professional advice.

Mentions of specific products or services do not constitute an endorsement or recommendation. The authors assume no responsibility for errors or omissions, or for any damages that may result from the use of the information contained herein.

Acknowledgments

The authors are grateful for the valued suggestions of Ava Anderson, Donna Anderson, Rondi Anderson, Shakti Anderson, James Chasey, William Costley, Dixie Watts Dalton, Holly Jones, Keller McCabe, Alexandra Morlote, Calliope Power, Kelsey West, and Jackie Zephirin.

Table of Contents

Chapter 1

While families in surrounding homes devoured chicken casseroles and air-fried meatballs, the shadow of a man darkened the lobby of the Green Oaks Public Library. The stout silhouette descended a back stairway and traversed a corridor that was once spattered with blood. Upon entering a small room filled with dusty, old books, the man removed a vial of red liquid from his pocket and set it gingerly on the table in the center of the room. He put a fresh straight blade on his scalpel. It would be a long night.

***

The following afternoon across town, Eloise stretched her arms above her head as she turned to look at her best friend.

"Bisa, what did you get your sister for her birthday?"

"My gift was a promise not to bug her until after dinner, but just on that one day!"

"Seriously, do you two exchange gifts?"

Eloise rubbed her palms along her blue jeans as she waited for her best friend to respond. Bisa always seemed to know what to do.

Afternoon sunlight trickled into Eloise's living room as the two sat comfortably on a beige shag carpet. Eloise thought it would take all the fun out of the event if she simply asked her little sister what she wanted for her 13th birthday in the coming spring. She wanted to surprise Dorothy with a special gift.

Eloise's house was unusually calm while the rest of the Alberty family was off getting lost in a corn maze that she had mastered during a school field trip the week before. Their absence gave Eloise time to hang out with Bisa without her brother and sister monopolizing the cozy living room.

Bisa and Eloise created mild mischief in that house as children. As high school students, competitive sports, stacks of homework, and broader social circles kept their previous boredom at bay. Eloise didn't mind a fast-paced lifestyle, but it did make her prize a rare lazy afternoon.

She tilted her chin up to the ceiling as a daydream transported her to a recent lesson in her economics class. Her favorite teacher had mentioned the high value often associated with things in short supply. When it came to appreciating a lazy day, the sentiment rang true. Still, she figured there must be more to it, because she only had one brother and she didn't value his infrequent fart jokes.

Bisa's laugh brought Eloise back to reality. "Our gift giving is pretty low key. I might do her chores for a day or buy her some junk food."

"My family is frugal with gifts, too," Eloise shared. "I like to bake my parents bread for their birthdays and give my brother something from the thrift store, if he's lucky. But I feel like going big for Dorothy's birthday. She's becoming a teenager and she really needs a good bike to get around on. She wants to start babysitting and her best friend just moved two miles away. If I start a job now, I'll have six months to save up money for it. She loves adventures and I want to help her go places."

"That would be so sweet of you! And a part-time job would give you work experience!

My mom keeps bugging me to build my resume."

Eloise tilted her head to the side, "What does that even mean?"

"Before you try to get a job, it helps to make this fancy summary of your accomplishments that you can share with potential employers. On my resume, I listed my job as a swim instructor and my leadership role as captain of the volleyball team. If you start working after school, that job will go on the list. We can also add our positions in school clubs and other extracurriculars that help us stand out. A strong resume can help you get your dream job someday!"

Eloise nodded her head. "I'm up for earning some extra cash and building my resume, I think. A super nice bike costs $400. That's a big commitment. Should I really do this?"

Bisa picked up a deck of cards and spread them around on the carpet like pepperonis on a pizza.

"Eloise, life is like a card game. You've only got 52 weeks each year, just like there are 52 cards in this deck. When you spend a week on something, it's like playing a card from this deck. Each card can be played only once. If you spend a week of summer vacation playing video games, you've played a card."

Bisa symbolically picked up a card from the floor and laid it on top of the game console nestled next to the television and continued. "That means you lose the opportunity to play that card with family, friends, school, or sports."

Bisa nodded toward the card, "If you waste a play, you waste your time, and you never get it back."

"I'd say I wasted the whole suit of diamonds daydreaming about Alex last spring," Eloise said, solemnly.

"A good play prevents us from missing out on important opportunities." Bisa picked up two more cards from the floor and held them in front of Eloise. "Those two weeks you spent at soccer camp instead of moping around the house were a good play."

Standing up, Bisa placed the two cards on the soccer trophy Eloise had resting proudly on the computer hutch. "The cost of that play was a missed opportunity to spend two weeks listening to your brother talk about his latest cooking catastrophe. My economics teacher calls the value of the next-best alternative that you give up when making a choice an 'opportunity cost.'"

Eloise chimed in, "My mom said Warren followed a taco-noodle-maple-syrup recipe he found online and the house smelled like gas for two weeks. My opportunity cost was low!"

Bisa sighed, "If only he wanted to make something delicious. I'd be here at dinner time myself if Warren made lasagna, and your opportunity cost of going to camp would increase because you'd miss out on something yummy!"

Eloise grinned and picked up a second deck of cards from her family's game shelf. "Okay, so spending two weeks at soccer camp left me with a missed opportunity to spend time at home. Spending money is a similar game, right?"

Eloise began dealing the second deck of cards out haphazardly onto the floor and saying, "money, money, money." She stopped and held a card in the air. "This card represents my spending money for the week. I can spend this money on a pizza or on a pair of sunglasses, but I can only spend it once. If I buy the pizza, the opportunity cost is the sunglasses."

To punctuate her point, Eloise sent the card spinning into the mauve sofa across the room.

"Exactly," Bisa confirmed. "To be precise, your life is like a game of Poker!" Bisa poked Eloise in the ribs with a playing card.

"Oh, yeah? Well your life is like a game of Crazy Eights!" Eloise laughed and tossed her remaining cards into the air.

Bisa threw a handful of cards at Eloise. "No, it's War!"

Cards fluttered from the sky like confetti and landed all over what had been a spotless living room.

Eloise laid flat on the card-blanketed floor. Sliding her arms and legs back and forth, she arranged the cards into a teenager-shaped angel. Sunlight reflected off the waxy surfaces of the playing cards and sent dim flecks of light dancing around the room.

Bisa suddenly got serious. She picked up one last card and gestured toward a photo of Eloise's sister on the TV stand. "Trying to save up enough money for an awesome bike will be a real challenge. If you ask me, working to buy Dorothy a special birthday gift will be time cards and money cards well spent!"

Eloise stopped flapping her angel wings and turned to Bisa. "Where did you learn to think about time and money as cards?"

Bisa shrugged as a mischievous smile inched along her lips, "Would you believe me if I took full credit?"

A momentary pause filled the room as the two friends looked at each other. Eloise erupted into laughter as she shook her head. Bisa admitted, "Yeah, you're right. My mom gave me the card example before I started lifeguarding. I guess the lesson stuck, since I learned it well enough to be able to teach it to you. I wish I could say the same for the swimming lessons I gave Tommy Bickle."

The two sighed and used their fingers to rake far-flung cards back into their boxes.

Eloise had no idea where her quest for a part-time job was about to lead her. Had she known, she might have baked her sister a loaf of bread instead.

Chapter 2

The school day felt longer than usual. The drama after the morning assembly didn't help. Principal Mayburn had lost her glasses and enlisted the entire school to join the search. Students scoured the campus of Green Oaks High School, mainly excited for the excuse to run wild. After 15 minutes, one of Eloise's classmates found the missing glasses sticking out of a flower pot just outside of the school's main office. Foul play was not suspected. Everyone knew Principal Mayburn liked to tend the flowers near the entrance before starting the school day.

Walking home after school, Eloise pictured Dorothy unwrapping a shiny red bicycle. The bike would come with a high-pitched bell that sounded like her grandmother's kitchen timer announcing that brownies were ready to eat. Upon glimpsing the tasseled handlebars, Dorothy would scream and call Eloise the best sister ever. Eloise grinned in anticipation of turning her daydream into a reality.

As she strolled down the sidewalk, Eloise realized that her financial picture was a fuzzy question mark. She hadn't kept track of her occasional cash gifts and earnings. How much money did she have? Maybe she only needed to work for a few weeks to pay for the bike? Eloise foraged through her backpack to find the smooth, yellow wallet that grasped her financial situation. She opened the little wallet and hoped for the best. A huff left her lips at the sad sight. Her idea of picking up a few extra babysitting gigs to fill the gap in her finances contrasted sharply with the paltry handful of crumpled dollar bills in her possession. The anticipated small gap in funds was, in reality, a gaping hole. Eloise repacked her backpack and sighed. She was tight on cash.

Eloise's only earnings came from shoveling snow and babysitting. Sadly, her spending kept pace with her earnings the way her hero, Hellen Obiri, kept pace with Brigid Kosgei when running a marathon–step for step. To bring her earnings ahead of her spending, she resolved to earn money faster by finding a better-paying job.

Someday, Eloise hoped to have money to burn. She sought the financial stability that allowed her parents to donate to the Green Oaks Animal Shelter and fix things around the house that were on the fritz. Eloise remembered how their failing refrigerator had turned her favorite popsicles into puddles the previous summer. The repairs weren't cheap, nor were recent car and gutter repairs. Even so, her parents were able to remedy the problems before they got worse. Eloise knew her parents invested many years of their lives into education and hard work to build that financial security. Secretly, she vowed to start building her own financial security, one addition to her resume at a time.

As her walk home took her under the colorful awnings of Green Oak's Main Street, Eloise sifted through a handful of job options in her mind. Being a high school student with limited experience, she knew her choices for part-time jobs weren't the best. She could probably be a sales clerk at the local mall, load boxes at the local sock factory, rent out shoes at the bowling alley, or flip burgers at the locally famous MacGreasy's restaurant. Eloise hoisted her backpack higher onto her shoulder. None of those options sounded right. Maybe she was missing something?

An impatient driver honked at a double-parked truck filled with flour for Leticia's Pizzeria. Turning her head toward the sound, Eloise noticed a green flier taped to a lamppost.

Drawings of books with happy faces on their covers drew her closer. She read, "Help wanted at the local library! Pays $13 per hour!"

Eloise looked across the street and smiled at the row of trees that hid the public library just out of sight. Feeling it was her lucky day, she dropped her book bag on the grass below the lamppost and studied the flier again, narrowing her eyes. She mumbled under her breath, "I'm going to need a resume."

Eloise made a mental note to pick Bisa's brain about how to perfect a resume. She really wanted to stand out from the other applicants and show the library she was serious about doing good work. She figured a strong resume would help tilt the odds in her favor.

Her mother liked to say that things have a way of working out. Eloise needed no more convincing because this seemed like the perfect fit. The library clearly needed workers and Eloise badly wanted work. Eloise became overwhelmed with optimism. Laughter bubbled from the back of her throat and morphed into excited hollers as Eloise jumped up and down. It wasn't the only time when the library would make her scream.

Chapter 3

Eloise knew her resume would be thin because she didn't have much work experience. It struck her that one's first resume presents a puzzle. If you need work experience to get a job and you need a job to get work experience, how do you begin? It made her think of the puzzle about which came first, the chicken or the egg. Eloise wondered if people with jobs forgot how hard it was to start. Why did so many jobs for beginners seem to want previous work experience? It almost felt unfair. Still, Eliose knew Bisa would know what to do.

In an evening summit on the Albertys' front porch, Bisa helped Eloise arrange her work-related experience on a single sheet of paper. They placed her past work experience at the top, her education in the middle, and her extracurriculars near the bottom. They emphasized her relevant skills, used strong action verbs, kept everything clear and concise, and proofread carefully.

Eloise thanked Bisa for her help with a large helping of homemade peach cobbler. As Bisa headed home, Eloise reread a portion of her resume with fresh eyes. Their wordsmithing had made her work babysitting and doing odd jobs for neighbors sound downright impressive. She read some of her favorite parts out loud.

“Supervised children aged 3 to 11 in their homes, ensuring safety, assisting with reading skills, and providing meals within dietary guidelines. Established positive relationships with children and parents through effective communication and trust-building.”

The descriptions sounded better than she had expected. She felt she had solved the resume puzzle: her resume contained the chicken or the egg, whichever came first.

Retiring to her bedroom, Eloise held her professional-looking resume up to her bedroom light for a last proud glance. Resting her masterpiece gently on her unmade bed, she clapped her hands together in satisfaction.

After school the next day, Eloise brought her application and resume to the library. The book drop box outside carried a sign welcoming job application documents. A small frown tugged Eloise’s eyebrows downward. She didn’t want her application to get wrinkled in a pile of books. Summoning courage, Eloise strode over to the library's wide wooden doors. She figured it couldn't hurt to go the extra mile when applying for a job. Luckily, in her case, the metaphorical mile was a mere 20-second walk from the curb into the library.

The aging brick building was a sight for sore eyes. As she followed a local shopkeeper through the creaky door that had seen better days, Eloise inhaled a deep breath of what smelled like old books and wood. Massive bookcases stretched towards the ceiling. Two comically tall and thin ladders dared to stretch the impressive distance between the ground and the top stacks. The sight reminded Eloise of a scene from one of her favorite fantasy books.

A woman with blonde highlights in her wavy white hair peered over thick-rimmed glasses at Eloise. "Hello. May I help you?" Eloise took in the woman's gold name tag, which read, "Mrs. Sophie, Head Librarian, Green Oaks Public Library."

Mrs. Sophie's knowing, wide eyes made Eloise wonder how many librarians were owls in a previous life. Eloise nervously licked her lips. She momentarily took a step back before changing her mind and offering Mrs. Sophie her hand.

Smiling, she said, "Hi, my name is Eloise. I came in to apply for a part-time position at the library."

Mrs. Sophie's blue eyes flickered as she exclaimed, "Wonderful. I can take your application."

Eloise could feel her heart pumping but she maintained her composure. "I saw that applications can be placed in the drop box, but I didn't want it to get wrinkled. First impressions mean so much."

"Oh, I couldn't agree more. I'll take a look at it, Eloise. Is your contact information on your resume?" Mrs. Sophie could tell from Eloise's guilty expression that she had not written down a phone number or email.

"Please write the best way to contact you on here." Mrs. Sophie offered a bright pink sticky note and a pen. Eloise wrote down her email address and cell phone number. She carefully placed the note onto the front of her application.

"Thank you, Eloise. I'll check it over and reach out to you shortly. Remember to include a good way to contact you on your resume. A job offer does you no good if you never receive it." Mrs. Sophie playfully waved the application in Eloise's direction and said goodbye.

Eloise walked toward Main Street and hiked her backpack onto one shoulder. As she admired the bouquets in the front window of the florist shop, a familiar chime danced into the air. She instinctively dug her phone out of the front pocket and answered, "Hello?"

"Hello, Eloise. It's Mrs. Sophie. We spoke a few moments ago."

"Oh! Did I forget to put something else on my resume?"

A lighthearted laugh sounded from the opposite end of the phone. Mrs. Sophie quickly replied, "No, your resume was great. In fact, I would love to hire you. Can you start this week after school?"

"Yes! Thank you!"

"Excellent. I'll email some details to you. See you soon."

That evening Eloise contemplated her possible work schedule. Dorothy's birthday had motivated her to earn money and her successful job search inspired her to think big. What else could she do with the extra income if she put in more hours?

Eloise's thoughts became shaped by the bright green leaves swaying outside her bedroom window. She imagined the leaves were money growing on trees. If they were, she knew several giraffes would be competing to eat the green leaves, each depicting a money-hungry activity standing in her future. One giraffe would portray the pizza party she was invited to that evening. Other giraffes on the horizon would represent the family lake trip for spring break, college, and, ideally, a car. She would need a lot of leaves or very disciplined giraffes.

Seeking to control one giraffe's appetite, Eloise told herself she didn't care what type of car she would own someday. Deep down, she really wanted a silver Mustang convertible with a brown interior and heated seats. A picture of that gorgeous car was taped above her bed.

Dorothy entered the bedroom she shared with her sister. Eloise was perched at the window. "Whatcha doing?" Dorothy inquired.

Eloise spun around and looked adoringly at her little sister. "Watching giraffes eat the leaves off our oak trees," she replied, wearing a grin.

"Um, okay. Did you see the new tree Mom planted next to our old sandbox?"

Eloise looked out the window and spotted the small, almost-leafless tree in the corner of their yard. It occurred to her that in the money-tree analogy, that seedling represented her current financial state. She would have to wait for leaves to grow on the tree before launching any sort of spending spree. Patience was not Eloise's forte. To be fair, the trait did not run in the family.

Eloise replied, "I hope it grows big enough to shed piles of leaves for us to play in someday."

"You watched that warm-and-fuzzy movie about the family that plays together in the leaves again, didn't you?"

A small grin inched along Eloise's lips. Her little sister knew her too well. Eloise simply nodded her head and shrugged.

Plates and cutlery clinked in the kitchen as Eloise's family prepared for dinner. Feet padded down the hallway and Maryam Alberty poked her head into the room, "Girls, will you help set the table?"

"Sure, Mom," they said in unison.

Eloise walked out of the bedroom, down the hall, and into the kitchen. Dorothy bounded a few paces behind with her pink hair ties swinging from one side to the other.

Dorothy folded her arms across her chest and pouted, "Mom, I'm hungry."

"Patience."

Dorothy rolled her eyes as she sat in her seat and listlessly swung her legs. She added, "You don't understand, Mom. I'm really, really hungry right now. I could eat an entire giraffe!"

The edges of Eloise's lips lifted into a smile. She placed a cup on her sister's placemat and asked, "Where's Warren?"

"He's at soccer practice. They're going a little late to prepare for their upcoming game. Don't worry, he's on dish duty tonight."

"Awesome." Eloise settled into her seat as Dorothy droned on about being famished.

Eloise looked at her little sister and teased, "You'd fail the marshmallow test."

"What's the marshmallow test?"

Eloise's mom was hovering over her daughters with her hair piled into a high bun. She jumped into the conversation, "It's a test of delayed gratification first conducted at Stanford University. The kids in the test were told they would get two marshmallows later if they could resist eating one for 15 minutes. It tested each kid's ability to wait in order to get what they wanted."

Dorothy mumbled, "I don't think I'd pass."

"Me neither," Eloise admitted, sending Dorothy a playful wink.

Inside, Eloise was upset with herself. She was willing to bet that, like many of the test takers, she would have eaten the first marshmallow without hesitation and later regretted losing out on the larger rewards. As evidence of that weakness, Eloise had contemplated spending what little money she had on unneeded food at the pizza party that evening with her friends rather than saving for bigger things later on. Eloise realized she needed to prioritize carefully when facing the tradeoffs of daily life. Was the pizza party her marshmallow?

Intent on playing her cards wisely, Eloise closed her eyes and contemplated her current options: outing, vacation, gift, college, car. The most current addition to the list weighed on her mind. The pizza party with friends sounded fun, but wouldn't that be a waste of money? Eloise turned towards the stove and decided to ask an expert. She knew her mother was an economics major in college and would have a few pointers.

"Mom, I need your help. I'm trying to save money. I just got a part-time job at the library, but my friends invited me to a pizza party tonight that would cost $15 or so. What should I do? Part of me feels bad for spending the money. It's not like I'll need more food after eating the dinner you're making for us. But part of me really wants to go out and have fun with my friends and I would feel awkward being the only person not getting pizza and a rootbeer float."

Her mom pulled a steaming lasagna out of the stove, "It's normal to see spending money tonight differently than spending in the future," Maryam assured.

"Most people discount future costs and benefits, treating them as smaller than if they were paid or received today. Impatience is one of the reasons for that discounting. Another is that we can't predict the future. Uncertainty about future costs and benefits can diminish their importance. If you save all your money for college and then end up getting a scholarship that pays for college, you'll wish you balanced your spending better. It also makes sense to discount the future enough to justify a reasonable amount of spending now, because your health might change. If you save everything for later, a future broken leg or zombie apocalypse might stop you from enjoying them as much."

"A zombie apocalypse?" Eloise smirked, surprised to hear her serious mother use such a silly example.

"Last weekend your brother asked me to watch another zombie movie with him. It's still rattling around in my brain." Maryam clucked her tongue in protest, adding, "But putting zombies aside, a recession, war, natural disaster, or global pandemic could have the same effect."

"Good point, Mom." Eloise stretched her arms. "I guess I'll go to the party."

Feeling heard, Maryam cautioned, "Just don't discount the future *too* much. Heavy discounting leaves way too many people unprepared for the days ahead. Time flies, Eloise. If you spend like there's no tomorrow, you'll be cursing your past self when tomorrow becomes today."

"My budget right now is really tight. How do I save enough to avoid regrets later and spend enough to avoid regrets now?"

Her mom laughed, "That's tricky. I'll tell you my approach. For starters, I chose my career and my employer carefully. Those decisions are down the road for you, but it's important to consider which jobs fit not only your passions and skills, but also your interests in financial stability, advancement, work-life balance, location, and job security. Different jobs have different workloads. I prioritized a job where I could work enough to avoid the constraints that come with a painfully tight budget. Sure, the job market has some say in the options available, but hard work in school and in early jobs helped me build a resume worth looking at. I don't love my job every single day, but it's a tradeoff to feel financially secure every day."

"It seems scary to start a career."

"It's an adventure, but things have a way of falling into place if you're well prepared and persistent. The job at the library sounds like a great next move."

Eloise scooped a generous helping of lasagna onto her plate just as the front door opened and Warren rushed inside. She waved to her brother and continued, "Okay, so once my budget is determined, what's the secret to spending wisely?"

"I can't tell you any secrets, but I can tell you a strategy. I like to start with today's essentials. We need a roof over our heads, food, clothing, medicine, and enough money to cover other important family needs."

"I think you should save money for family needs by making Warren eat dog food."

Warren tossed a baby carrot in Eloise's direction. She bobbed to the left and the carrot landed on the floor.

"Keep your brother out of this," Maryam said sternly, failing to hide a smile.

"Next, I think about future essentials. We must set money aside for upcoming necessities like utility bills, mortgage payments on our home loan, property and income taxes, and insurance payments."

"Sounds important."

"Third on my priority list is a rainy day fund. Things don't always go as planned, so it's wise to save up for unexpected expenses. Remember when a certain someone kicked a ball through our front window last summer?"

Eloise nodded as Warren grumbled between bites.

"The money for the new window came from the rainy day fund."

Eloise shoved broccoli around on her plate. "I really like the idea of a rainy day fund. I guess I shouldn't go out tonight, right?"

"Well, hold on. As a teenager, your rainy days aren't as expensive as they will be when you have your own household. Still, making a small rainy day fund would be smart."

"I've got $50 in my sock drawer," Eloise whispered, leaning away from Warren.

"I heard that," Warren announced, "But it was only $47.50, and I spent it all on an ice cream maker at Jerry's yard sale." Sensing anger about to explode all around him, Warren quickly added, "Just kidding!"

Maryam continued. “Priority four is important stuff like education or training for your career. You don’t need those things to stay alive, but they will change your life for the better. So, you need a plan for how to cover those costs. The plan might include loans and work-study along with savings, but you need to have a plan.”

“Work study?”

Maryam nodded, “Work-study offers eligible students part-time jobs. The program aims to help students with education-related costs while also giving them job experience.”

“For sure. Are we getting to the part where I go to the party?”

“Yes. The remaining decisions are between less-important stuff now and less-important stuff later. The goal is to enjoy today without sacrificing your ability to enjoy tomorrow. When deciding between putting money toward savings or making a not-so-important purchase now, ask yourself how the purchase would affect your future. If it would put you into debt or prevent you from paying for something with a higher priority, you risk losing something important to your future, and it's probably not the best idea to spend that money now."

"I'm glad I asked. With my rainy day fund in place and my job at the library lifting my budget constraint, going to the pizza party tonight seems like a good way to balance enjoyment now and later."

"Agreed!"

Warren looked over at Eloise and asked, "Wait. You got a job at the library?"

Chapter 4

Eloise looked in the mirror one last time. She narrowed her eyes and tried to figure out what was wrong with her outfit. Dorothy walked into the room and looked over her big sister's clothing choices.

"Shoes," Dorothy blurted out as she plopped onto her twin bed. Her cheerful floral bedding sharply contrasted with Eloise's dark blue comforter.

Eloise frowned and turned toward the bed. Dorothy's face was already buried in a chapter book but she felt Eloise's glance and replied to her big sister's unspoken question.

"You're wearing two different shoes."

Eloise looked down at her mismatched brown boots and mumbled, "Oh, thanks."

"Hey!"

"What?"

"If you come straight home after getting pizza can you please grab me a slice? I think I saved up enough allowance money to pay you back." Dorothy's eyes were so large and excited that Eloise refused to say no. Buying an extra slice of pizza wouldn't exactly ruin her budget. Eloise had built enough cushion into her new budget to account for random unexpected expenses like food for a hungry sister.

Eloise turned to her little sister and playfully tapped Dorothy's nose. "Sure thing. Don't bother paying me back. It will just count as your next birthday present."

Dorothy jumped forward and swiftly waved her hands in the air like a soccer referee indicating a disallowed goal. "No! I don't want to have pizza as my next birthday present."

Eloise felt bad as she watched her sister's panicked expression. She quickly soothed, "Hey, I was just kidding. I'll do a little better than a slice of pizza when your birthday arrives. Sorry for the bad joke. And I'll still bring you back a slice."

"Thanks, Eloise."

"No problem, Sis."

Dorothy reached over and tossed Eloise's tan cropped jacket into the air. Eloise caught it as she headed out of the bedroom. "Thanks!"

"Congratulations on choosing a jacket that actually matches your boots!"

"Very funny!"

A now-matching pair of boots clomped down the hallway as their mother called out from the living room, "Why all the yelling? What's going on?"

Eloise snorted out a laugh as she paused next to the front door and replied, "Nothing, Mom!"

A tiny voice from down the hall agreed, "Nothing, Mom!"

Excited for the night to come, Eloise headed to the party at Leticia's Pizzeria. The scents of grilled burgers and the sounds of joyful nightlife mingled on Main Street in the Saturday evening air. Eloise breathed it all in, feeling better about her future. Talking to her mom earlier that day had boosted her confidence about financial choices. Together, they had ranked the importance of potential purchases and carefully crafted a budget that would prevent overspending on low priorities. Even though Eloise didn't always feel like it, she was pretty young. She didn't need to know everything. It was enough to think carefully and ask plenty of questions.

"Eloise!"

One of her friends waved her over. A bright grin spread across Eloise's face as she returned the gesture. It was time to balance her hard work with play time with her pals.

Chapter 5

As Eloise's girlfriends dove into a hamburger pizza, she shared her big news. "I got a job! I'm going to work at the library." She didn't get the cheers she expected.

Her friend Lily awkwardly stirred the contents of her root beer float with a straw. After a brief pause, Lily spoke through half-chewed pizza. "You know it's haunted, right? Ever since the murder in the basement."

The other friends nodded knowingly. A few people near the back of the long table had the good sense to look down at their phones to avoid offering an opinion on the matter.

"That was many years ago. Surely it's safe now," Bisa asserted in the library's defense.

Jackie gestured at Eloise with the tip of her pizza slice. "You shouldn't ever go into the library basement. No joke. My uncle lives across the street from it and he says that, late at night, a dim light appears in the basement and he sees shadows moving down there. I bet it's the spirits."

Eloise wasn't sure what to think. Half of her wanted to believe they were messing with her. Unfortunately, the other half wasn't so sure. Green Oaks was a small town that felt safe, but that didn't mean creepy things couldn't happen there. Just because everyone knew your name didn't mean the sleepy community held no secrets. Maybe she'd accidentally stumbled into a literal skeleton in the closet.

A thrill raced down Eloise's spine at the hint of an upcoming adventure. Her friends didn't understand her love for a good mystery. Their warnings put a spark in her eye. Eloise couldn't help it; she was curious.

"I'll take that into consideration, ladies." Eloise nodded, before changing the topic to their favorite high school teacher, Mrs. Gardner, who made all of her own clothing.

As Eloise walked home after the party, she placed Dorothy's carefully wrapped pizza slice in her purse and plucked her phone from her back pocket. The last thing she wanted was pizza grease all over her purse while her rainy day fund had no budget for a new one. She thought back to the conversation about the murder and the mysterious light. She couldn't wait to sort fact from fiction about strange events in the library basement.

She put Google on the case. Eloise wondered if the local news sites had any stories on a murder in the library. By the time she got home, Eloise's fingers felt numb. Her furious typing felt useless. She'd found a handful of gossip on local websites mentioning the legendary haunted library. None of the stories talked about anyone's untimely demise.

The library building was actually warm and welcoming, though quirky. It was old and slanted at an odd angle. Its warped shingles and chipped bricks didn't exactly convey an elegant image. Eloise reasoned that just because something was old didn't mean it was haunted. She had enough aging possessions to know that. Her phone was an older model and its screen looked like it had been through an animal attack, but it didn't seem haunted in the least. The phone did contain an inexplicable number of software bugs, but that was a mystery she'd need the phone techs in the mall to solve.

Sitting at her desk, Eloise gently flopped her phone into her lap and sighed. "I'm missing something." She tapped her cracked phone screen and thought about her next move. How could she find the answers she was looking for?

For some reason it felt like she was looking in the wrong direction. Dim lights and shadowy movements would not make the local news, but a death in the library's basement would. Maybe she just needed to type in the right keywords.

Eloise closed her eyes and imagined the predicament like a math problem. How could she rework the problem in front of her? Did she need to start from the beginning or was she simply missing a step? Maybe she'd overlooked something.

Eloise tried a new approach to her murder investigation. She opened her laptop and logged into the library's online database. The computer dutifully whirred as she entered her password and waited for the search page to load. The library had a search engine dedicated to old "archived" newspaper articles. She leaned her head to the left as she sorted keywords in her mind. She typed, "murder green oaks public library basement."

Within seconds, her computer brought up images of yellow crime-scene tape wrapped around the front stairs of her new place of employment. The old photo from the Green Oaks Gazette was taken 21 years prior. Eloise groaned when she realized the article that went with the photo had not been digitized for the online database. Her small town didn't have the resources to pay someone to scan and upload all of the old print articles. Talk about time-consuming tasks.

Sleep danced near the corners of Eloise's eyes after countless hours searching down another online rabbit hole. She knew it was best to stop for the night. Still, she itched to learn more. The only things stopping her were her mounting exhaustion and burning eyes. She'd look again in the morning, she thought, turning away from her laptop.

With all of her thoughts revolving around the Green Oaks Public Library, she instinctively reached into her purse to retrieve her new employee's library card. A rush of pride filled Eloise's chest as she admired the symbol of her new role at the library and her first step toward financial security. A photo of the sprawling oak tree near the library's entrance filled most of the card's front side. Her own photo rested within the top of the tree's branches while her name and employee number sat below the roots. She had climbed that tree as a child, although she remembered it having more branches. Feeling dead tired and ready to collapse, it occurred to her that old, dead branches that had broken off the tree lost the privilege of appearing in the photo. They had become woodchips spread around nearby flowerbeds, which gave her a thought.

The local news coverage she was searching for did not live on the internet, but those old stories still existed and were scattered elsewhere. The date on the crime scene photo gave her a new lead. With an exact date of the crime, she could look up bits of information in the fully digitized archives of larger newspapers elsewhere.

Eloise chuckled as she thought back to the countless times she'd visited Lily's house for dinner. Lily's mom was the most popular news reporter in town. Her dinner conversations, like her news stories, were an unnerving mix of exaggerated "puff" pieces and heart-pounding crime stories. At least meals at Lily's house were never boring. Thanks to Lily's mom, Eloise felt confident she understood a little bit more than the average teenager when it came to the media. One clear lesson from those conversations was that big-city newspapers have an "if it bleeds, it leads" policy that assures coverage of an intriguing murder in a small town.

A half-hour later, Eloise had found ample news stories to confirm the gruesome events in the library basement. Lily was right about the murder. A banker named Donovan Brie was found dead in the basement room where the library kept a collection of historical financial records. His body was pinned under a fallen bookcase as if it had fallen on him. The police suspected foul play.

Eloise read several retellings of the incident and learned that the death looked intentional due to the way Donovan Brie's head rested on the carpeted floor. A few clicks later, Eloise found confirmation in the autopsy report published a week later that Mr. Brie had received multiple blows to his head from a pointed object. The same week, a news story broke that surveillance videos captured a disgruntled bank patron following Mr. Brie from the bank to the library. Soon after that, a librarian reportedly found blood on the corner of an old metal box of index cards.

Eloise shook her head at her computer screen and sighed. Her unexplained mystery suddenly felt a lot more real.

The sequence of news stories helped Eloise piece the deadly episode together. Mr. Brie had caught a bank customer wrongfully transferring funds from his employer's bank account into his personal account and turned him in. The angry embezzler followed Mr. Brie to the unmonitored records room in the library where the banker went to look up old deeds. After hitting Mr. Brie in the head with the corner of the metal box, the killer laid a large bookcase on top of him to make the death look accidental.

Convinced that her online sleuthing had caught her up on that dark day 21 years ago, Eloise pulled herself back into the moment. She turned off her laptop and phone. Staring at the blackened screens, she wondered if reading too many grim tales could twist her perception of reality. She vowed not to become paranoid.

Maybe she'd start hearing more fascinating things about the library now that she had taken interest in it. She'd noticed that phenomenon before. When she started thinking about attending Centre College after high school, it seemed like she suddenly saw ten times as many people wearing Centre College sweatshirts. She hoped the world was giving her a sign that she was heading in the right direction. More likely, it was the world showing her that you miss a lot when you're not paying attention. She closed her eyes and hoped to learn more scoop on the library soon.

Chapter 6

In Monday's economics class, Eloise learned that 700 million people in the world live on less than $2.15 per day. Her gratitude swelled for all that she possessed. Her parents had bought her a phone and a laptop to help with school. She had to share the laptop with her little sister. Lucklly, Dorothy wasn't too interested in the online games that kept many computers hostage for hours on end. In return for her phone, Eloise did the dishes on weekends, washed her family's clothes twice a week, and took out the trash every Tuesday. Well, she used to.

Knowing her talent for penny pinching, her parents made her an offer. They would take over her trash duties on Tuesdays if she could find them a better phone plan than her mother had found. It was the perfect incentive for someone who loved to find a bargain and didn't love trash.

Eloise hadn't known anything about phone plans or payments until she started looking. The first plans that popped up in an internet search were no better than what her mom had found. Eloise couldn't believe how much people were expected to pay for a so-called bargain. She persisted, digging for lesser-known companies intent on luring in customers with irresistible prices. She scrolled past the sponsored links and read a ton of reviews. Her shopping around paid off. She found a plan with glowing reviews that provided off-brand phones and unlimited service for $9 less per month than their previous plan.

The same persistence that helped Eloise find a better phone plan propelled her through the school day. As she descended the front steps of Green Oaks High School, Lily patted her shoulder from behind. Eloise turned to see her friend wearing purple overalls and a concerned look. “I told my parents about your job at the library. My dad says strange things are still happening there.”

Eloise stopped at the sidewalk and subconsciously crossed her arms. She was excited about her job and didn’t welcome bad news. “My dad walks past the library very early on most mornings. He has to be at the bakery by 4:00 a.m. to get the dough rising.”

Eloise suddenly realized how hungry she was. Lily continued, speaking louder than necessary.

"My dad said that on mornings after fresh snow falls during the night, there is often a single trail of footprints leading out of the building."

"Oh, didn't I tell you?" Eloise asked. "I figured out that each night at midnight, a new zombie hatches from a giant egg in the library basement and makes its way downtown to devour unsold bread left in the bakery dumpster."

Lily wasn't amused by the attempt at humor. "I'm just sharing information. Be careful, Eloise." "I'll try not to jar the eggs," Eloise replied. "And my shifts end by 9:00 p.m., so I should be safe." The two parted ways, neither pleased with the conversation.

After dinner, Eloise took Warren's call for a belching contest as a clear sign that, instead, it was time to study for her upcoming math midterm. Retreating to her bedroom, she sat at the small desk she shared with Dorothy.

She heard a few distant belches and decided to close her door. The silence of her room allowed Eloise to unwind from the chaotic day. She hopped onto her twin-sized bed. Above her on the wall, a local pop band's poster of three horses playing guitars curled near the edges. Eloise wondered if she'd eventually be able to afford tickets to see her favorite band. Thanks to her new job at the library, she felt one step closer to those types of dreams. For now, she needed to focus on saving her money.

Her mind drifted back to schoolwork as she pulled out some handwritten class notes. Her loopy cursive was interspersed with numbers and printed letters. She liked writing in cursive because the motion felt faster than printing. Eloise also enjoyed how neat cursive made her notes look. Someday she would sign checks, contracts, and other important documents with the finest cursive signature around.

Math class that day had covered simple and compound interest. Her teacher, Mr. Schnell, loved story problems. Eloise tried to focus, but thoughts of a midterm sent her heart racing. She liked being at the top of her class. What if the new information wouldn't stick?

Eloise pushed her notes away. She closed her eyes and sucked in a big gulp of air. She had so much to focus on at the same time. Between saving up for Dorothy's birthday, hanging out with friends, working at the library, and keeping her grades up, Eloise felt like she barely had a second for herself. Maybe she just needed to take it one step at a time.

She took a deep breath, exhaled, and whispered to herself, "You've got this."

Her self-confidence pushed her forward. She remembered all the times she had worried a lesson would be difficult. The material only seemed scary because she hadn't learned enough about it to feel in control of the situation. Most of the time, the hardest part of studying was simply starting. Maybe the same would be true for solving the mystery of the lights and shadows in the library basement.

Eloise opened her eyes and pulled the pile of notes closer. She crossed her legs and grabbed a new pencil. She decided to read the homework questions out loud. She took inspiration from Bisa, who swore that her brain understood things better when she both read them and said them. Bisa always got the best grades in math class.

Eloise looked over her homework and read out loud, "How much more interest would Wesley's

Worm Farm earn in one year on its $10,000 bank deposit if the interest were compounded monthly rather than yearly?"

Eloise knew the answer was that she didn't care about a worm farm. She looked over the question and wondered if she could apply the same concept to her life. Eloise was curious about how much she would have to put in a bank today to have $400 in six months. That would be enough to buy Dorothy's bike. She opened her laptop to do some personal finance sleuthing. Eloise discovered a bank would pay interest on the money she deposited into a savings account, meaning a certain percentage of her deposit would be added to her account as a reward for holding that money in the bank.

She then searched a local bank's website to discover how often the bank would compound interest. A tiny detail near the bottom caught her eye. She read the fine print and grinned. The bank compounded interest monthly, meaning it paid interest each month, and the interest percentage was always applied to the initial deposit plus whatever interest had accumulated so far. The bank's annual interest rate was four percent.

She flipped her notebook to a blank page and wrote “4% annual interest rate compounded monthly.” Eloise wanted to solve her own problem using the new skills she had learned in class.

Eloise mouthed her personal word problem, “How much does Eloise need in the bank today, earning four percent annual interest compounded monthly, to have $400 in six months?”

Mr. Schnell had taught her the formulas for simple interest and compound interest. With simple interest, the interest rate applies only to the original deposit. So the amount accumulated is simply the amount deposited plus that amount multiplied by the interest rate times the number of years it was deposited. Or, as Mr. Schnell liked to write on the chalkboard, an amount $X deposited for N years at annual interest rate R would accumulate to:

$$\$X + \$XNR = \$X(1+NR)$$

Eloise took a breath and tried to remember the formula for compound interest. She turned to Felix, her old teddy bear. Felix had seen better years. His once brown fur was fading to white. Eloise didn't mention Felix to her friends, but she still kept him on her bed. The little bear was important to her.

She cleared her throat and poorly imitated Mr. Schnell's nasally voice. "With compounding C times per year, an amount $X deposited for N years at an annual interest rate R grows to this amount." Eloise wrote the formula on her whiteboard:

$$\$X(1 + R/C)^{N \times C}$$

"So, Felix, since my bank compounds interest 12 times a year, C is 12, and we know R is four percent or 0.04. N for me is 0.5 because I have one-half year to accumulate $400. So simply plug those numbers into the formula and set it equal to $400." She wrote on her whiteboard:

$$\$X(1 + 0.04/12)^{0.5 \times 12} = \$400$$

Eloise wrinkled her nose as she concluded her impersonation of Mr. Schnell, "Solve for $X and we see I need to deposit $392.09. Yikes." The whiteboard held the evidence.

$$\$X = \$400/(1 + 0.04/12)^{0.5x12} = \$392.09$$

Eloise put her pencil down after showing Felix her problem. She looked at him for a moment and laughed. She was sure he knew all the answers but wouldn't share them. He wouldn't be of much help for her larger problems unless he was stuffed with cash.

She grabbed Felix and held his face up to hers. "Look, Felix. We've solved one puzzle just to have another appear. I was hoping interest payments would help fill the gap in my savings, but they don't amount to much when the money's only in the bank for 6 months!"

Eloise glanced over her homework and sighed. "Time to start looking for better solutions."

Chapter 7

Eloise felt elated to start her first job. She wanted to make a strong first impression, even if her task that day was sorting large piles of books into small subject categories for shelving. The rows of shelves seemed to stretch forever. Eloise perused the fiction section, wishing she had enough time to read every one of those books. She could always give the monumental challenge a try during her breaks and days off.

A smile crept along Eloise's lips as she bent down to extract two misplaced books from a bottom shelf. A book about astronomy had no business sitting next to a book dedicated to taxes, and there they were sandwiched between *The Firekeeper's Daughter* and *The First Paper Cut*. From the dust gathered on both spines, it didn't take a detective to see that they had been hiding on the fictional mystery shelf for a great while.

How many people had passed over books that they wanted to read because the novels were hidden in the wrong place? How many times had Eloise been unable to find the right information because she was looking in the wrong direction? The outline of an idea hovered in the back of Eloise's mind but she couldn't seem to fully grasp its meaning. She held the misplaced books tighter in her arms and tried to give her unformed theory time to develop.

Eloise's new co-worker, Cali, brought her more books. "Sorry to add to your pile, but these were in the basement." Her curly brown hair bobbed around her shoulders as she carried an impressive stack of hardcovers.

"No worries." Eloise grabbed a few books from the growing mountain beside her and methodically returned them to their rightful places.

Cali leaned over a pile of jumbled books and teased, "I bet you didn't see this coming on your first day."

"Not really, but I wasn't sure what to expect. So far, I like working at the library."

"That makes two of us." Cali stood on the tips of her toes and tried unsuccessfully to place a book on the top shelf.

Eloise moved from one foot to the other as she tried to figure out what to say. She didn't want to seem rude by making insinuations about Cali's height, but she also knew it was unkind to ignore a coworker in need.

"Can I help with that?" Eloise's voice sounded more uncertain than she'd intended. She hesitantly held a thin paperback between her palms as she waited for Cali to respond.

A throaty chuckle wheezed out of Cali's throat as she lowered her weight back onto the balls of her feet. She held her hand up disapprovingly and explained, "Thank you, but I have this under control. I'll be right back with a small ladder. We usually keep them near the front desk in case you need to use one in the future."

"Thanks." Eloise nodded and returned her attention to the stacks of unsorted books. She could almost swear the pile was getting larger by the minute. She knew it wasn't possible, but the thought danced in the back of her mind as she leaned over a worn blue hardcover.

As she strained to read the handwritten Dewey Decimal Classification number on the book's little white sticker, a small note slipped from between the pages and fluttered to the floor. She remembered her mother's stories of passing notes with her classmates hidden inside of books. Eloise wondered if she'd accidentally discovered a piece of paper detailing some past math class gossip. She eagerly reached down and flipped over the note to reveal its message.

As the words registered in her mind, her mouth dropped open with a soundless scream. She held the note with two hands and read it out loud, "COVER MR. BROWN'S SPINE BEFORE STARTING OUR PERFECT MURDER."

Eloise's thoughts traveled to black and white horror movies where monstrous people sold body parts in underground markets. She held the note several inches away from her face as she worried over its meaning. Who was Mr. Brown? Where was the rest of his body?

Eloise could tell the offending piece of scratch paper was fairly new. Well, new compared to some of the aging books in the town library. Maybe this note held the key to why everyone seemed to think the library was haunted.

Decidedly, Eloise spun toward the front of the building and took the note to her supervisor, Mr. Ducat. She weaved between half-empty reading tables and marched around an old, wooden book cart. Seeing her pass, Cali could tell Eloise was on a mission.

Mr. Ducat was easy to find. He liked to sit just to the right of the front desk. His nose was buried in a book about fossils as she approached. "I found this in a book that Cali brought up from the basement!"

With trembling hands she slapped the note down in the center of Mr. Ducat's desk. Eloise realized she was yelling and overcorrected to a whisper. "It's about a murder and, and hiding body parts."

Mr. Ducat glanced up from a page about trilobites. His wide-brimmed glasses rested halfway down the bridge of his nose. Reluctantly, he nudged an unfinished crossword puzzle to the side of his desk to clear space for the small document of interest. He studied the note through his thick bifocal glasses.

Eloise waited for him to gasp or turn pale. After a few seconds, Eloise wondered if the scream had simply lodged in the back of his throat. Clearly, he wasn't very good at showing his emotions.

"Well?" Eloise prodded as she instinctively stepped away from the desk. "Should we call the police?"

Mr. Ducat looked back at his book and spoke in a monotone voice. "There was one murder in the basement that permeates local lore, but that was 21 years ago and the case was solved. There is no harm being done in our basement, and if this note has anything to do with a murder in our library, then it's about a closed case."

"But this paper doesn't look that old. What if there are more murders that haven't been discovered yet?" Eloise quickly added, "Have you been down there recently?"

"Yes. It is a wholesome space. You have an overactive imagination, that's all I can say."

Eloise didn't know whether to consider her supervisor's response suspicious or simply dismissive. She wrinkled her nose, straightened her spine, and leveled her gaze with Mr. Ducat's.

"Perhaps," she stonily replied. As Mr. Ducat studied the remains of insects trapped in tree resin 40 million years ago, Eloise grabbed the note from his desk and dutifully returned to her sorting tasks.

Eloise couldn't get the alarming note out of her head. She had spent countless hours watching amateur detectives skulk around on one of Dorothy's favorite television shows. Eloise didn't know much, but she knew it was important to trust her gut. Right now, her gut said to keep digging for more clues. Besides, if Mr. Ducat turned out to be right, it would just mean the library was much safer than most people thought. To her credit, Eloise knew better than to let her questions get ignored. Just because Mr. Ducat worked at the library, it didn't mean he knew everything that happened there at every moment of the day. To some degree, Eloise didn't like Mr. Ducat's response because she felt like she wasn't being heard.

Eloise contemplated the risks and uncertainties of being a sleuth. Her mother had taught her about the dangers of uncertainty and the possible rewards of taking calculated risks. Maryam claimed that lessons about handling uncertainty applied far beyond the financial world. Eloise closed her eyes and wondered if she could apply some of her mother's lessons to her predicament over the grim note.

Maryam had described the rewards for investments in terms of the "rate of return," meaning the net gain over some period–usually a year–measured as a percentage of the amount invested.

For example, if a $100 investment had a 10 percent annual rate of return, the investor would have $110 after one year. She would have the $100 she invested plus 10 percent of that $100, which is $10. Eloise's parents took risks by investing in the stock market, where the average rate of return was higher than the interest rate they would receive on money placed in safer places, such as a savings account at a bank. But they cautioned that the "risk premium" of that additional return investors expect to receive, on average, from stocks came with the possibility of losing the whole investment.

"Don't invest more in stocks than you can afford to lose," her mother had advised, "and diversify by choosing a variety of investments. A mix of stocks, bonds, and certificates of deposit, or CDs for short, can be good. If you're investing in stocks, you can get diversity by investing in an index fund. That type of investment fund simply replicates the stocks in one of the stock indexes, such as the Dow, the Nasdaq, or the S&P 500. Diversification reduces the risk of a big loss caused by the failure of one company that you've sunk a lot of money into."

Eloise rubbed the bottom of her neck as she applied lessons about diversifying risk to the mystery in the library. She wasn't investing money, but she was investing time, which had some value as proven by her $13-per-hour wage. Eloise knew she faced uncertainty about the note, the basement, Mr. Brown's spine, and potentially at least one more murder. She doubted Mr. Brown was still alive given the ominous words scrawled across the note.

Eloise went straight home after work. She was thirsty for answers, but for the moment would have to settle for a seltzer water. She hummed pensively as she opened the can and emptied its contents into a tall glass of ice. Was Mr. Ducat involved? What if Cali was also in on it? Was a lone figure dissecting bodies in the library's basement? Was the note related to the murder that happened 21 years ago? Or was she entirely off base? A tornado of unanswered questions whirled around in Eloise's mind as she took another measured gulp.

She thought of the classic game of *Clue* in which players tried to determine who, where, and how crimes occurred. If she were playing that game in the library, she would have accused Mr. Ducat of murder in the basement with a cleaver. Yet, she knew her mom would equate such a narrow accusation with putting all of her money into one stock. If Eloise invested all her time into one theory and it was wrong, her stock would crash, and her time would be wasted. Eloise knew her mom would encourage her to diversify her theories, at least until she had more certainty about some of them.

She faced additional risks as well. If she pinned it on Mr. Ducat or Cali or anyone else and had it wrong, she would surely lose her job, not to mention her reputation and her pride. She certainly didn't want to hurt anyone's reputation if they were innocent. Eloise ably tossed the seltzer water can into the recycling bin across the room. She knew making strong claims without proof had the potential to get good people into trouble, including herself.

Determined to act wisely, Eloise headed out of the kitchen with a new plan in mind. She would diversify by investing time into each reasonable theory. Her first step would be research to narrow out unlikely bets. The theories that felt more likely would earn more of her time.

Eloise turned off the lights above the kitchen cabinet and muttered, “Time to diversify my interests.”

Chapter 8

Eloise woke up feeling invigorated. It was Saturday and she had sleuthing and book stacking to do. She packed a snack and headed over to the library. The warmth of the sun felt comforting against the back of her white sweater. She inhaled and prepared to set her new plan into motion. Her boss was unconcerned and uncooperative. Maybe that was useful information. She would just narrow down her suspicions, pursuing one theory at a time. Her favorite working theory? Mr. Ducat was totally guilty.

The front steps of the old library came into view as Eloise rounded the corner of Poplar Street and Vine Street with unusual speed. She tripped over a rock and barely regained her footing. Eloise wondered if she had the right target for her investigation. What if everything she had observed had a perfectly reasonable explanation?

As she approached the library, a curtain covering one of the basement windows swayed. Eloise stopped in her tracks. She squinted and tried to make out shapes behind the curtain. Maybe the air conditioner was still on full blast. The sudden movement could have been nothing, or just the clue that she was looking for. The chilly morning air felt ready to turn warm as the sun's first rays danced along the grass. Eloise huffed as excited knots twisted and turned inside of her belly. She took a measured step forward and prepared to face her second shift at the library.

Once inside, the smell of old books greeted Eloise's sensitive nose. She spotted Cali behind the front desk and waved. Cali pushed away from the computer and smiled. Her hair stood in every direction as she shook out her curls.

"Hi, Eloise! I didn't know you had a shift today."

Eloise hoisted her backpack slightly higher on her shoulder and grinned. "I asked to take a Saturday shift. I'm trying to save up enough money to buy my sister a bike for her birthday. Besides, the library is a great place to study during my breaks."

Eloise tilted her head to the side and looked at Cali. She needed to consider her new friend as a possible suspect until she had more clues. For now, she couldn't rule out the theory that

Cali knew about the fate of Mr. Brown. Eloise wondered how she could test the theory. Maybe she should ask Cali a few questions.

The crime novels and detective shows had never talked about this specific situation. How could she indirectly ask someone if they were involved in a library-wide murder coverup? How could she ask questions without looking suspicious? Maybe casual conversation would provide enough clues to improve her working theory.

Cali grinned as she walked around the front desk to meet Eloise in the lobby. She held a small envelope out to Eloise.

“What’s this?”

Cali kept the tiny white envelope extended. Mischief sparkled in her gaze as she bounced on the heels of her feet. Slowly, Eloise accepted the mysterious envelope and looked inside. Handwritten notes on paper scraps filled the inside of the envelope. Eloise looked up at Cali. Then her gaze traveled to the few members of town brave enough to enter the haunted library. Eloise’s shoulders relaxed once she realized no one was looking. She pulled out one of the small pieces of paper and inspected the note.

“Be sure to put Mr. Twist back in his place.”

Cali leaned forward and whispered, “I heard you found an odd note in one of the books during your last shift. I wanted to show you the ones I’ve found over the last few months. I haven’t kept all of them, just the really weird ones.”

“Over the last few months?”

“Yep. I try to inspect the books before putting them back on the shelves.”

Eloise’s fingers twitched around the envelope as she processed Cali’s words. After a beat, she realized at least one of her theories felt less likely compared to the rest. It sounded like Cali was just as eager to put together the clues as she was.

“Thank you, Cali. I can’t wait to read them over.”

“Knock yourself out. I’m so glad you’re working here. You’re really kicking up the dust around this old place.”

“I hope not in a bad way.”

Cali’s laugh made a mirthful sound like twinkling chimes, “No, you’re giving this place new life. It’s no fun being stuck here with Mr. Ducat all day.”

For once, Eloise could agree. The man was less than pleasant when it came to listening to her concerns. It made Eloise feel good to work with someone like Cali who could hear and address her questions. While Mr. Ducat was an avid reader, his ability to relate to other people felt wanting. It was a point that stuck out to Eloise as she built her case. Maybe her Saturday shift would be a lot more fun than expected.

Her optimism changed when she saw that Mr. Ducat worked on Saturday, too. She decided to steer clear of him as much as possible, which lasted about a minute. As she squinted to read titles on a top shelf without pulling them down, Mr. Ducat came up behind her. “Eloise, I’m sorry if I was brisk with you yesterday. I’ve been kind of moody. I'm facing some problems at home."

"I'm so sorry to hear that," Eloise responded reflexively. She added, "Is your family okay?"

"Yeah, it's really just me and the cats in an apartment, but I may be going bankrupt. It's a long story, but it has me agitated much of the time. Between that and my landlord hounding me about rent payments, I'm struggling a bit. Sorry for the drama."

"No need to apologize. Good luck sorting things out."

Eloise wondered whether Mr. Ducat realized he was acting suspiciously and needed to come up with an explanation. He was no help at all to her investigation. He didn't even acknowledge the possibility that there was reason for concern. Cali shared that Mr. Ducat had mentioned his possible bankruptcy to her, too. It might have been an excuse for his behavior, but it wasn't new and perhaps it was true.

After walking home from her Saturday morning shift, Eloise pulled out her laptop and embarked on another deep dive into the internet. Energized by her encounter with Mr. Ducat, Eloise decided to investigate what it could mean for her boss to face bankruptcy. She figured a good online search was like detective work–she needed to ask the right questions to make the investigation productive.

After a few minutes, she discovered six different types of bankruptcy. Each was named after the chapter that defined them in the U.S. Bankruptcy Code. Eloise pushed back from her laptop and processed the new information, "So there are different types of bankruptcy?"

Eloise had thought that bankruptcy was a blanket term meaning financial trouble. It wasn't so simple. According to the web, most people filed for something called Chapter 7 bankruptcy. That helps eliminate certain debts that a person cannot fully repay. Examples included credit card debt, medical bills, utility bills, and past-due rent payments.

Eloise wondered whether bankruptcy was an easy opportunity to escape from debts. She wandered out of her room and found her mother sitting on the couch in the den. Maryam's head tilted down as she perused a crossword puzzle.

"Mom, why doesn't everyone just buy their home and car with a loan and then declare bankruptcy?"

Maryam tucked her feet under her legs and smiled. "It doesn't work that way. Home and car debt can be erased, but typically those loans come with the condition that the lender gets the car or home if they are not repaid. Bankruptcy doesn't change that. So if you get out of the debt, you're also out of the home and car. If you rent your residence, you might be protected from eviction for 30 days, but then you'll probably be kicked out if you can't catch up on your payments."

These answers multiplied Eloise's fascination with the concept. New questions flew into her brain and out of her mouth. "How about loans for school? Could students take advantage of bankruptcy? Can I take out student loans and then declare bankruptcy?"

"I'm not sure where these questions came from, but I like your curiosity. Bankruptcy usually does not eliminate student loans. It also generally doesn't apply to unpaid taxes, money owed for drunk driving incidents, or debts for child support or spousal support, among other things. Usually bankruptcy is thought of as a last resort. Think of it as an attempt to save a sinking ship. It's a last-ditch effort that doesn't end well for anyone."

"But if you owe money on a credit card, it gets you out of that?"

"It might, but like I said, bankruptcy is really a last resort. In some situations, a court appoints someone called a 'trustee' who oversees the sale of your assets to pay off your debts as much as possible."

"So if you end up in bankruptcy, you're out on the streets?" Eloise asked. "I know people talk about it on the news, but I didn't know it was so scary." Eloise's mom frowned as she patted a couch cushion. Eloise sat down, and her mom grasped her hand.

"Thankfully, no. The laws vary by state, but there are exemptions that allow you to keep the things you need most. Exemptions can include medical supplies, clothing, and household items such as dishes and furniture. You might also be able to keep your car and home if you're able to keep up with your loan payments on them. But even though you keep some essentials, bankruptcy is complex and requires you to pay whatever you reasonably can. After bankruptcy, it's usually hard to get another loan, at least for a year or two."

"Yuck. I can see why Mr. Ducat is so moody. He's stressed about maybe having to file for bankruptcy. He also said something about his rent payment being a problem. Is a rent payment the same thing as the mortgage payment I've heard you and Dad talk about for the house?"

"No, there's a difference. You pay rent to the owner of something in exchange for being able to use it. Paying rent doesn't help you become the owner. Our mortgage payment helps us become the owners of our home. That loan helped us buy the house when we didn't have enough savings to pay the whole price. We make a payment each month. Part of it goes toward the amount we borrowed, which is called the principal. The rest goes toward the interest we pay on the loan. After we pay the loan off, we will own the home."

"So you pay interest to the bank to compensate them for using their money, like the bank will pay me interest to compensate me for my enormous deposits someday?" Eloise asked.

"Right. And the bank can lend the money from deposits like yours out to people like me for homes like ours. The bank's profit comes from the difference between the interest rate they pay you for your deposit and the higher interest rate they charge borrowers like me," her mom explained.

"That makes sense. And rent is different because it's not repaying a loan?"

"Exactly. Mr. Ducat's apartment is owned by his landlord, and the rent is a monthly payment to his landlord for the use of the place."

"I'm kind of following, but why would someone rent a place instead of making what might be a similar monthly payment in order to eventually own the property?"

"Good question. There are several reasons some people prefer to rent. Renters have fewer responsibilities for the property and its upkeep. They have the freedom to leave when their rental period ends without having to worry about selling the place. And renting doesn't require a large upfront payment called a 'down payment' which banks require before they'll provide a loan for the rest of the cost of a home."

"Gotcha. So when I'm in college, it will probably make sense to rent because I won't have a lot of money for a down payment, and I'll want flexibility without having to be responsible for things like repairs."

"Precisely."

"But if I get enough money later on and find a place where I want to live, it might make more sense for me to take out a mortgage loan and buy a house."

"I can't wait to visit!" Maryam said, gleefully.

"Very funny, Mom. You'll need to wait a little longer. I'm still working on the whole school thing."

"I know you'll continue to crush the school thing." Eloise's mom patted her daughter's hand. With a few more answers under her belt, Eloise stood up from the couch and headed back to her room.

The conversation with her mom helped Eloise better understand Mr. Ducat's financial struggles. He was definitely in some type of mess. Eloise wondered how deep Mr. Ducat's troubles ran. Somehow, he had gotten behind on rent, and although he could file for bankruptcy to discharge many of his debts, he might lose his apartment and the ability to borrow money for a long while.

Eloise looked at her stuffed friend, Felix, and announced, "I'm starting to feel sorry for Mr. Ducat. I'm mean, unless he's a murderer."

Chapter 9

Eloise sat on a wooden bench in the school cafeteria and watched Bisa finish a rectangular slice of cheese pizza. It wasn't bad for school food. Eloise liked to get a slice of mushroom pizza on the rare days when she was too busy to pack a lunch. Today, Eloise's bologna sandwich with mustard was a gooey mess.

"Bisa, I may not be headed to bankruptcy like Mr. Ducat, but I still have money issues of my own."

"Yeah, I get it. We're just starting to work and save up for things. Luckily, I've got the secret sauce for your savings!" Bisa said between bites of pizza crust.

"Whaaat? You have some kind of secret?" Eloise said with a giggle.

"Okay, it's not really a secret. Maybe it's more like magic, and it's definitely underappreciated and underused." Bisa playfully wiggled her eyebrows as she placed the crumpled napkin in the middle of her tray.

"What's the magic, Bisa?"

"The magic of technology will make your savings grow. The library can directly deposit your paycheck into your bank account. The people in the banking world call that a 'direct deposit.' When you fill out the direct deposit form for the library, you can request that part of your paycheck go into your checking account and the rest into your savings account. It's a great way to automatically add to your savings. The money never touches your hands and tempts you by calling out, 'buy a concert ticket with me!'"

"I'm in! Do I need both a checking account and a savings account?" Eloise asked.

"Yep, it's a good idea to open both. You won't get much interest from the checking account, but you'll have an unlimited number of transactions. You can take money out using an ATM, short for Automated Teller Machine, checks, or a debit card. Unlike a credit card, a debit card pulls the money straight from your checking account."

"So maybe I don't need a savings account?"

Bisa rattled her tray as she shook her head and explained, “A savings account is nice because it usually pays a higher interest rate. It also helps you separate your savings from your spending money. A disadvantage is that you generally can’t draw directly from a savings account with checks or debit cards. But you can access your savings with an ATM card or by visiting the bank, and you can transfer money between your accounts online. They have phone apps for that. Some banks limit the number of times you can transfer money out of a savings account each month, but it's usually about six times. I don’t really touch my savings account, so that’s plenty for me.”

“Thanks, Bisa. I’m glad your parents work for a bank!”

“Haha. Very funny, but it is helpful information when trying to start saving up.”

“I’m sold,” Eloise confirmed. “I’ll get a checking account for easy access and a savings account for higher interest rates. I like the idea of separating my money into a checking account for money I can spend sooner and a savings account for money I’m holding onto until later.”

"One more thing. When you choose your bank, check into the fees they charge. Banks charge fees for things like checks written for more money than you have in your account, called overdrafts, accounts with low balances, stuff like that. Many banks are trying to be more competitive by lowering their fees. Still, you have to shop around. Fees can bite hard if you don't watch out for them! Look for a fee-free account!"

"Fee-free is for me." Eloise laughed at her friend's seriousness. She was glad Bisa, with the help of her parents, was able to teach her a little about the financial ropes.

Eloise added, "Now I need to figure out how much to set aside from each paycheck for Dorothy's bike." She looked at the cloudless sky as she mulled over her options.

Bisa pulled out a ripped piece of scratch paper from her math binder. "Let's break down the math."

"Sure. I have 20 weeks before I need to buy the bike. I get paid every 2 weeks. So I have 10 more paychecks. The bike is $400, so I need to set aside $40 each paycheck for the bike," Eloise calculated.

"Exactly. And you're working 10 hours a week for $13 per hour, so each paycheck is two times 10 times $13, or $260. That means you'll have $260 minus $40, which is $220, left over from each paycheck to buy dresses for your best friend."

"You bet, Bisa, right after I save enough for college, a car, and a house."

The bell rang, and the duo cleaned up their usual lunch spot. Kids slowly returned to class. Eloise couldn't wait for the dismissal bell to ring. She had a new mission to complete.

After school, Eloise arranged to meet her mother at the Green Oaks Bank and Trust. While some online banks offered accounts that required no minimum balance, Eloise opted for a bank with a physical location just down the street from her school. For her, it felt like the simplest choice that worked best for her current needs.

After her deluge of questions about the bank's fees and policies, the teller joked that Eloise was not only ready to bank there, she was ready to work there. She would need her mother to be a joint owner of the account until she turned 18. They charged no fees for opening or maintaining a basic checking and savings account. If she bounced a check, meaning she wrote it for more than her checking account balance, she would pay a fee of $20 plus a possible fee from the business she wrote the check to. Eloise planned to keep careful track of her balance to prevent that.

Feeling satisfied that she wouldn't be hit with unexpected fees, Eloise provided the $50 minimum initial deposit and opened her savings and checking accounts.

Eloise was filled with pride as she left. She finally had a place to stash her hard-earned future earnings. From the extra bounce in her mother's step as she split off in the direction of her office, Eloise felt sure that Maryam was proud, too.

Chapter 10

Eloise kicked her feet over the side of Bisa's treehouse. They used to climb up here all the time. She remembered when it felt like they were miles away from the ground. Now, the ground was a brave jump away, a subtle reminder of how quickly time moves.

"Bisa, I'm having trouble juggling all the drama in my life. I'm pretty sure there's a murderer in the library's basement, I have a math test coming up, and all this talk about finances is stirring me up."

Bisa wiggled her toes over the edge of the treehouse, showing off coral-colored nail polish. The two watched from the front yard as the occasional car drove down Bisa's street.

"You're overthinking all of this. Try breaking it down. We don't know for sure that there is a murderer in the basement. It could be a lot of things. Maybe there's a light on a timer that's gone awry."

"That doesn't explain the shadows," Eloise noted.

"Maybe Mr. Ducat likes cats so much that he hides one at work that occasionally triggers a motion-detection light and makes shadows in the night."

"Perhaps, but if that's the case, he's doing a nice job smuggling in the bags of cat food and kitty litter he'd have to bring every so often."

"Hmmm. Yeah. About school," Bisa continued, "I know you'll rock the math test."

"Thanks for your vote of confidence. Rock might not be the right word for what I'll do, but I've studied so long for that test that my score should be solid."

"Don't worry about the finance questions. I can help, and my parents know a ton of that stuff! Like Mr. Schnell says, learning anything is mostly about devoting the time, focusing, finding the motivation, and choosing the right sources."

"For sure. By the way, thanks for teaching me about savings accounts. Are there any better ways to start saving? I feel like I'm starting a marathon that everyone else is already running."

"Not to brag and all, but I can help you take control of your finances. Listen and learn!"

"Show me the money!" Eloise said enthusiastically, knowing Bisa loved that line from the old *Jerry Maquire* movie. Bisa made a hobby of referencing classic movies whenever she could. Eloise secretly thought that her friend would have an amazing career as a film producer.

"Okay. After listening to my parents talk about banking for about a million years, I can definitely give you a quick summary of some of their favorite investments. Let's talk about certificates of deposit, which are also called CDs. These are on the safe side of investments and generally pay higher interest rates than savings accounts. You can get them from a bank or credit union when you're 18 or older. Depending on which type of CD you choose, you need to keep the money invested for a period that's usually between three months and five years. If you withdraw your money early, you pay a penalty. The penalty is usually several months' interest."

Eloise mulled over Bisa's explanation and shrugged. "Safety sounds good to me! And

Mom mentioned CDs a while back when she was telling me about some different types of investments."

"Yes, but remember the trade-off between risks and rewards."

"I know," Eloise said. "In the card game of life, there's always a tradeoff. Give me your quick summary of an investment opportunity that's a bit more risky and might offer higher rewards."

"Sure," Bisa responded. "When you're 18 you can buy bonds, which are a type of loan. When you buy a bond, you're basically lending money to the seller of the bond. You give them some money, and they give you an IOU in the form of a bond. Many corporations, colleges, and governments sell bonds to borrow money for whatever they're up to. Bonds can be riskier than CDs, and may offer a higher rate of return. Are you still following?"

Eloise nodded, "Still following."

"When the period of the loan is over, the bond 'matures.'"

"I was hoping that would happen to Warren at puberty, but no such luck."

Bisa hid a smile. "At maturity, if all goes well, the issuer of the bond will pay you a predetermined amount called the 'face value' of the bond. That is, unless they run into financial trouble and can't pay you, in which case they 'default.' As an example, you can buy a U.S. Treasury bond with a face value of $1,000 which will mature in twenty years."

"Okay, let me see if I understand. So if I buy a bond that matures in twenty years, I get the face value in twenty years unless the issuer defaults. If the issuer defaults, then my investment is in trouble."

"Right. And bonds from the federal government are considered pretty darn safe. The default risk is higher for companies."

"Gotcha. And the far-off maturity dates explain why my grandma bought me a Treasury bond when I was a baby to help with college expenses twenty years later. That bond had a twenty-year maturity date. Now it finally makes sense!"

Bisa added, “Bonds also pay a type of interest rate called a ‘coupon’ rate every six months.”

“Okay, so you make some money along the way that rewards the purchase of bonds. Is the price I pay for a bond equal to its face value?”

“Sometimes, but if the interest rate paid on competing investments such as CDs is higher than the coupon rate on the bond, the initial price will be below the face value to make the bond an attractive investment.”

“Okay, you lost me a bit,” Eloise sighed.

“No worries. Think about my Aunt Donna. She owns a dairy farm right? Suppose other milking cows sell for $1,000, but Donna has a cow that produces less milk than the other cows. Can she sell it for $1,000?”

“She’d have to sell it for less because its milk production is lower.”

“Right. And a bond that’s producing less money due to a lower coupon rate will have to sell for a lower price, too.”

"Bisa, that makes sense! And I forgot your aunt had a farm."

"Yeah, it's fun to visit on weekend trips. Now, if my aunt has a cow that produces more than other cows, what can she charge for it?"

"A higher price."

"Yes! So likewise, if the coupon rate on a bond is higher than the interest rate on other investments, the initial purchase price can be higher than the face value because people will pay more for that bond to get its high rate of return."

"What if someone doesn't want to wait decades to sell their bond?" Eloise asked.

"An investor can typically sell a bond before it matures. However, there may be a fee for that sale, and the price received for that bond may be lower than the face value."

Eloise frowned. "What would make a bond's price go down?"

"Bond prices tend to move in the opposite direction of interest rates. If interest rates rise, fewer people are interested in bonds because money in CDs and savings accounts is earning more interest than before. As the demand for bonds falls, bond prices drop until they are competitive as an investment. Bond prices are affected in the same way by the rate of return on other investments such as stocks. And as the bond approaches its maturity date, its price tends to get closer and closer to its face value. Between the initial purchase and maturity, the bond may sell for a price above, below, or equal to the face value of the bond."

"I'm starting to understand. Also, you really sound like a banker right now. Let me see if I get it. Does that mean if you hold the bond until maturity, you avoid the risk of price fluctuations but still face the risk that the seller defaults and won't be able to pay you back?"

"Yep. And it's not very likely that a strong government will default, but companies do fail. If you want, you can buy U.S. government bonds at TreasuryDirect.gov when you're 18."

"You're filled with information! I'll look at that site later. So many age limits! I'm glad I'm almost 18. What about stocks? Stocks are more of a roll of the dice, right?"

"Yeah. Stocks are like partial ownership in a company. They are risky because their price depends on the performance of the company. If the company does poorly, the value of your stock goes down. If the company goes out of business, the stock can become worthless. That's why you want to make a variety of investments to kinda spread out or 'diversify' your risk."

"That's what my mom said. I've also heard that stocks can be expensive. Can someone with only a small amount of money to invest buy stocks?"

"Actually, it is possible to buy a 'split' or fractional share in many stocks, which helps make them more accessible."

"Good to hear! My mom also said something about index funds?"

"Yes, that's an easy way to diversify. You can also consider a mutual fund, which is a combination of investments such as stocks and bonds that a professional money manager puts together. But remember, you can lose money on all these investments."

"If I wanted to invest a little money in stocks–as my mom says, not more than I could afford to lose–how would I buy them?"

"You would open a brokerage account, which is free, but ..."

"But I'd have to be 18?"

"Right. It's also good to get plenty of practice on a stock market simulation before risking real money. They're easy to find online. Those software programs give you a chance to learn about the markets and try out strategies using play money. Once you're ready, if you're under 18, a parent or guardian can open a custodial or guardian account for stocks, bonds, or CDs. The adult manages the account until you're old enough to take over."

"So many options, Bisa! Where should I put my money?"

Bisa pursed her lips and raised her eyebrows. I wouldn't start with stocks. That's a good way to lose your shirt if the market crashes. It's better to start with lower-risk investments. The savings account was a great start. My parents always say not to rush into anything risky. They have stories about people they met at the bank who made bad investments and dug themselves into a hole."

Eloise grumbled, "If that's the case, then I'm scared to start."

"Just start small, safe, and slow."

"Easy for you to say, I need $400!"

"Feeling rushed will only add pressure and make it harder to make smart investment choices. Play it safe, Eloise."

Eloise fought against rolling her eyes. She was grateful that Bisa had taken the time to help her. Eloise knew she tended to want things right away. She wanted the library mystery solved yesterday, and she wanted to know all the information for her upcoming math test immediately. Eloise decided to counter the risks of her problematic impatience with Bisa's small, safe, and slow strategy. To be safe, step one would be research.

"Thanks, Bisa. Time to talk to my parents!"

Chapter 11

At breakfast the next morning, Eloise knew she needed to talk to her parents about money. She appreciated Bisa's input, but her parents had more experience, and she would need their help if she wanted to open a custodial bank account.

She sat down next to Dorothy at the breakfast table. "Mom, Dad, I'd like to start saving for college. I've done a lot of research and I'd like to make a very low-risk investment."

"Murilo, it sounds like our daughter is becoming a financially responsible young woman!" Eloise's mom said as she wrapped an arm around her husband and chuckled. He took a generous gulp of his black coffee and replied, "I never doubted her for a minute."

Eloise's mom sent her a proud wink. It was as if Maryam had already known what Eloise planned to say. Dorothy munched on her toast and doodled on her notepad, ignoring most of the financial jargon being tossed around the table. Still, she managed to look up from her food and multi-colored paper enough to enjoy the family time.

Eloise's points about the need to save money for college, a future car, and an unspecified special gift were well taken by Maryam and Murilo. Before a single bowl of cereal was empty, Eloise had successfully talked her parents into opening a custodial account. With that, Eloise could invest $250 of her earnings into a CD.

The school day was a blur. Eloise felt good about her persuasive skills after negotiating the custodial account with her parents. During lunch, she met Bisa at the salad bar and proposed a serious snooping mission at the library.

"The weird stuff happens at night. We've got to get over there after dark to document what we see and hear," Eloise said, wide-eyed.

Bisa replied, "I could go at nine o'clock tonight. It will be plenty dark then. Hopefully we'll catch the ghosts frolicking about. Or do they just sit around reading ghost stories?"

"Very funny."

A gentle look overtook Bisa's features as she amended, "Look, I'm just kidding, but I'm a little bit scared. This might be the most exciting thing that's happened in our little town in years. I've watched enough ghost-chasing TV shows to at least be curious about the whole thing. Maybe the ghosts aren't reading books in the library, but there's only one way to find out what's really going on."

"Thanks, Bisa. You're the best. Meet me at my house at nine?"

"Wouldn't miss seeing a ghost book club for the world."

That night, Eloise and Bisa drove over to the library in the blue station wagon Eloise borrowed from her father. She appreciated that her parents trusted her enough to use the car every once in a while. The car was just what they needed for a late night library stakeout.

They found a parking spot a half block from the library's darkened exterior. As they approached the building in silence, a dim light slowly came into view in one of the basement windows. Without saying a word, Bisa and Eloise looked at each other in amazement and then turned back to the window. Eloise stopped in her tracks, grabbed her friend's hand, and started running back to the car.

Bisa huffed, “Why are we running away? You’re allowed to be at the library. You work there!”

“Yeah, but didn’t you see the curtain move in that basement window? Someone or something probably saw us sneaking up!”

“How could they have seen us? It’s dark, and there are only a few street lights on. By the way, are you sure you never tried out for the track team?”

Eloise tightened her grip on Bisa’s hand as they maneuvered around a low tree branch competing for space over the sidewalk. She knew her friend was a nervous talker.

Bisa wheezed as she tried to keep pace with Eloise. “Would ghosts get upset about us sneaking around? Isn’t that their thing?”

Without dignifying Bisa’s questions with a response, Eloise hopped into the driver’s seat and motioned her friend into the car. After pulling out of the spot where she had parallel parked, Eloise attempted a three-point turn to reverse the car's direction and head home. Her turn was too wide and she scraped the car's front wheel hard against the far curb.

Bisa yelled, "Oh!"

A grinding sound told them the wheel's rim had battled against the curb and likely lost. For a moment, it sounded worse than nails against a chalkboard.

Eloise cringed at the sound, but knew she'd only scratched the car. No other property or people were harmed. She was still embarrassed about the accident, and Bisa felt shocked by the drama of it all. Neither of them spoke as Eloise drove home with renewed caution.

When they pulled into the driveway, Bisa jumped out of the car first and bent down to inspect the damage. Reluctantly, Eloise joined her friend and held her breath as she examined two angry scuff marks on the left front wheel's rim. Eloise's father would not miss something like that.

So much for a good day of sleuthing. Eloise wondered if it was possible to go into a situation feeling too confident. For once, she wished she had played things safer.

Bisa asked, "Let me guess, You're going to tell him?"

Eloise groaned, "Yep. I need to say it now. It will only get more complicated if he finds out later. Besides, he's my dad. He's pretty fair."

Bisa nodded, "I know. Sometimes I wish that our dads would switch places."

They found Eloise's dad doing situps on the living room floor. A trickle of sweat trailed down the side of Eloise's neck. She wondered how her dad was less out of breath than she was.

"We have bad news and worse news," Eloise said, hoping her father's exercises had him in a sympathetic mood.

"The less-bad news is that a rogue curb attacked the rim of one of your wheels. To be fair, I might have provoked it. Sorry. I will pay for the damages. The worse news is that there is definitely something weird happening in the library basement, and it isn't a yoga class."

Eloise's wit mildly soothed the situation. She decided that putting both stories together was the best way to share the news. Bisa and Eloise stood near the door while Eloise's dad contemplated the information. His eyebrows were practically in his hairline.

"Maryam is canning apples in our basement, which is hopefully less haunted than the library's basement. Why don't you share the news items with her, and I'll take a look at the car and visit the library to see if I see anything nefarious."

"Thanks, Dad. Be careful at the library. We'll go downstairs and tell Mom."

Bisa winced as she offered a small, "Hi, Mr. Alberty. Sorry about the car."

"It sounds like it's not a big deal. Mistakes happen when we're learning. It's part of the process. Thanks for being honest about it."

Eloise's cheeks felt hot as she exited the room and walked downstairs. Bisa followed a few steps behind. The sight of jars and the smell of sliced apples greeted Eloise's senses. Her lower lip momentarily twitched upward as she noticed a figure bent over a table.

"Hi, ladies. Want to help?" Eloise's mom held up two empty cans.

They badly wanted to can apples rather than share their news, but they filled Maryam in.

Meanwhile, after going outside to examine the car, Murilo drove over to the library. He had always dismissed the rumors about the library being haunted, but when his own daughter reported oddities in the basement, he felt it was worth looking into. He circled the building on foot, holding a flashlight in one hand and a large stick in the other, just in case. He checked for broken glass in the basement windows and looked for other evidence of a forced entry but found nothing suspicious. The lights inside the library were off, and he saw no motion in the seemingly abandoned building. He shook his head and went back to his car.

Once home, Murilo advised Eloise and Bisa to follow up with a body shop and Mr. Ducat. "Car insurance won't pay for the repair because our insurance has a $500 deductible, meaning we pay the first $500 of a repair. This should cost less than $500 to fix."

"Dang about the insurance," Eloise muttered. "And dang about the ghosts or whoever is in the basement. We must have scared them into hiding." Eloise tried not to sulk about her dad not witnessing any of the clues.

Before Bisa left, they looked up tire shops that could fix the rim. They narrowed it down to two shops that had favorable reviews online. Customers wrote about fair prices and quick service. Fair prices were what Eloise was looking for.

The next day they took the car to both tire shops to get estimates. The best price was what one body shop described as "only" $200 to fix the damage. "Only" was not the word Eloise would have chosen. That was about half the price of Dorothy's bike. She couldn't justify cutting into her recently-opened college fund to get back on track for a birthday gift, and her rainy day fund was too small to fill the gap. Eloise stared at the blemishes on her dad's car and decided to brainstorm new strategies. How could she pay for the car while also staying on budget for her sister's gift? She had some thinking to do. She also had some pressing questions for Mr. Ducat.

Chapter 12

Eloise rarely drank coffee because she thought it tasted like warm dirt, but her adrenaline rush from the light in the basement and the accident felt like a double shot of espresso. Unable to sleep, she obsessed over what evil dwelled in the library at night. Maybe there was truth to the gossip and ghost stories. She wondered if most of the missing people cases in the area could be traced to that basement. How long had the library played a key role in the dangers lurking around town?

Restless, Eloise turned over in bed and noticed the time. She couldn't believe it was almost midnight. Her mind raced about the footwork she had ahead. Her next shift at the library couldn't come soon enough. She needed to look for clues and she needed to earn more money. She was $200 short for Dorothy's bike thanks to her driving mishap. With her budget slashed in half, Eloise wondered if she should consider a cheaper bike. The $400 bike might not be in the cards.

Moving slowly to avoid waking Dorothy, Eloise pulled her laptop out from underneath her bed and looked into bikes she could buy within her remaining $200 bike budget. She clicked on a few kid's bikes and groaned. The reviews were not good. Even the top-ranked bikes priced at $200 or less had reviews that averaged three stars out of five. Eloise strongly preferred items rated four stars or above. Three stars? Eloise didn't want to open her wallet for that. She decided to check a few more sites. After half an hour, she had learned that the less expensive bikes were reportedly less safe, less reliable, and harder to fix than the bike she had originally planned on.

"That's not going to work," Eloise sighed. She didn't want to give Dorothy something of lesser quality that was more dangerous just because it fell within her crunched budget. Maybe Dorothy would like a different gift just as much as a bike?

Eloise tapped her fingers against the side of the laptop. The bright screen cast a glow around the dim bedroom. She didn't want to keep the screen too bright for Dorothy to sleep. She was also concerned that her parents might still be awake. They were big on making sure everyone got enough sleep and never overlooked light seeping under her bedroom door. Just to be safe, Eloise got up and placed a pillow near the gap at the bottom of her door. "Perfect," she said to herself. Now she could do more research.

Eloise considered the alternative gifts she could buy for $200. What if she divided that money somehow between two other things her sister liked: art supplies and potted plants? Dorothy was always creating something. She loved painting pictures of insects' faces magnified 100 times their actual size. Eloise admired her little sister for often giving her paintings as random gifts. At least once a month, Dorothy handed Eloise a new painting or drawing. Recently, the art pieces focused on grasshoppers and ants.

The large canvases for Dorothy's amazing artwork cost $30 each. Dorothy also loved potted plants, and dreamed of putting them all over their home. Potted plants cost $20 each at the local garden center. Eloise wondered what combination of the two items would cost a total of $200 and make Dorothy as happy as possible. She remembered her economics teacher describing the solution to this type of puzzle as "maximizing utility subject to a budget constraint." Eloise figured some reasoning would get her closer to the best solution to that puzzle.

Eloise knew the first canvas and the first plant would be treasured, because Dorothy needed and loved both items. As Dorothy got more of either item, that item would be needed less, so the value to Dorothy of another of the same item would go down. This, she remembered from class, was the story of "diminishing marginal utility." One moral of that story was memorable: It's often better to have a mix of the things you like, rather than a lot of one of those things, because the last few units of the abundant item are generally valued less than the first few units of something different. So, although potted plants were cheaper than canvases, Eloise felt confident she should mix in a few canvases, because the first opportunities to paint would make Dorothy happier than the last of many plants.

Eloise looked over at her stuffed study buddy, Felix, as she mimicked her father, "Maximize the bang per buck!"

She thought back to last summer, when she received the more nuanced version of his reasoning in a candy store in Lambsburg,

Virginia. Eloise had decided to spend $15 of her trip allowance on sweets. She was struggling to choose the best possible mix of candy and bubblegum with that budget.

Murilo went into full dad mode and explained, “I’m going to tell you how to get as much happiness as possible out of your money. You want to buy whatever gives you the most bang per buck. Think about the ratio of benefit to price. Maybe your favorite chocolates cost twice as much as the other candies. They’re still the best choice if they make you more than twice as happy as the other stuff. You probably also value variety, so keep grabbing chocolates only until you have so many that another would not give you more happiness per dollar than the other options. That is, stop adding chocolates when one more would not give you at least twice as much happiness as the candy that costs half as much. Then, start adding whatever other thing gives you the most bang per buck–maybe sour candies–until even more of those would not give you the most bang per buck. Keep selecting items based on benefit per dollar until you’ve spent your entire budget, and you’ll maximize your happiness.”

After her dad's little speech in the candy store, her mom felt compelled to add, "By the way, as you're thinking about candy purchases, don't completely overlook other consequences, like future cavities and an aching tummy."

With their more recent discussion about spending and saving fresh in her mind, Eloise had a better understanding of Maryam's point: Don't discount future costs, such as tooth and tummy pain, excessively.

Eloise applied her father's bang-per-buck strategy to reason through the best mix of canvases and plants she could buy instead of a bike. Canvases were one-and-a-half times as expensive as plants. To provide more bang per buck than a plant, a canvas would have to give Dorothy more than one-and-a-half times as much happiness as a plant. For the first canvas, Eloise felt sure that was the case. Dorothy would get a big thrill out of being able to create a new painting. Absolutely. She rarely got canvases because they were so expensive.

How about if Eloise bought her a second canvas? Yes. Eloise thought a second canvas would also give Dorothy more than enough happiness to justify the higher price. A third canvas? No. Eloise thought Dorothy would be considerably less excited about more painting after filling two large canvases, and that buying enough plants to fulfill her dream of making the house green was a preferable use of the remaining money. If Eloise was correct, the best way to spend $200 on canvases and potted plants for Dorothy was to spend $60 on two canvases and the remaining $140 on seven plants.

The plants and canvases seemed like great gifts. The challenge was making sure Dorothy got as much happiness out of the gift budget as possible. It wasn't exactly easy to know her sister's level of joy from each item. She just hoped she knew Dorothy well enough to be close with her estimates.

Still, Eloise had shiny bike spokes spinning in her head. She envisioned Dorothy biking down the sidewalk and laughing the entire way. For some reason, the idea of getting Dorothy a bike just sounded better. Maybe she'd pick up a few extra shifts at the library and be able to pay for the $400 bike.

It was comforting to have the canvases and plants as a backup plan that matched her current budget. She rubbed her eyes and turned off her computer. She needed to catch some sleep before school.

Chapter 13

All too soon, Eloise was in math class, struggling to tune into Mr. Schnell's lecture.

"Remember class, the math midterm will include story problems similar to the ones in your homework. Practice the homework questions diligently to make sure you understand how to apply the concepts."

The bell rang and students sprang out of their seats. Eloise stuffed her pencils back into her backpack and huffed. Sure, it made sense to study the homework questions, but what if she needed more practice? Where could she go to find more questions? She wanted to ask the teacher, but by the time other students finished talking with him, it was almost time for her next class. As Eloise exited the classroom, Bisa bumped her shoulder and asked, "What's got you too focused to notice your friends?"

"Sorry, Bisa. I need more practice questions. I've read the explanations of this stuff in the textbook but I feel like it's not clicking right now."

Bisa nodded as she gulped down half of her water bottle. She closed the lid and concurred, "You're right. This is just like the time when I couldn't follow a recipe for enchiladas. There's nothing worse than staring at instructions and not understanding what they mean. Maybe you can find better explanations?"

"Exactly. I remember that! You couldn't figure out how to fold in the cheese."

"Not to save my life. But now that I know what to do, it's easy. You put the cheese in the sauce pot and stir from the bottom up to mix it into the sauce."

Eloise snorted, "Yeah, but the first time you grabbed the cheese with your hands and tried to fold it in half."

Bisa shrugged as they reached a juncture in the hallway. Bisa turned left toward her English class as Eloise continued straight toward her gym class. Before Bisa disappeared from sight, she hollered, "It beats not trying."

Eloise hefted her backpack a little higher on her shoulder. "True that."

***

After school, Eloise's walk to the library felt longer than usual. She was in a funk about her homework. Maybe she'd be able to speak with Mr. Schnell tomorrow before math class. She wanted to keep her grades up and felt like she needed more help in math than the lecture and textbook could provide. Some kids had tutors or went to study sessions after class. She wanted to try more problems on her own before looking into tutoring. Besides, how could she afford a good tutor when she already needed to pay for the car and Dorothy's present? Eloise scoffed and figured her parents would help pay for a tutor if her last-ditch study efforts didn't give her confidence.

"Good afternoon, Ms. Alberty," a chipper voice called from the front desk as Eloise entered the library. Mr. Ducat lowered his reading glasses and observed Eloise from a distance. He arched a brow as he observed her worried look.

"Is something wrong?"

Eloise was puzzled by Mr. Ducat's nicer than usual demeanor. He normally huffed and puffed all day. Eloise took a beat to relish his sudden kindness.

"Kind of." Eloise admitted. "I'm having trouble learning a lesson in math class. I have a massive test in a few days, and I'm unclear on the material. I feel like I need more practice problems or a different approach."

Mr. Ducat sat silently in his little chair as he listened intently to Eloise's problem. Then he slowly stood from the chair and declared, "I think I might have a solution."

"Really?"

"Maybe. Have you used the new library annex?"

Eloise repeated, "The library annex?"

Mr. Ducat picked at invisible lint along his brown cardigan. "I'm going to assume that's a no. Follow me. I understand if you didn't know about it. We don't have the budget to advertise."

The two walked through the fiction section and came to a small alcove filled with laptops in mint condition. Stained glass windows invited multi-colored rays of light to enter the cozy nook. Eloise couldn't believe she hadn't noticed the area before. In her defense, her work reorganizing books and cleaning dusty shelves kept her where the books lived when she wasn't talking with Cali or Mr. Ducat.

"It looks amazing!" she exclaimed.

Mr. Ducat nodded as he pressed a few keys on the closest computer. He affirmed, "It better be. The town gave the library a generous amount of funds to update our educational resources. We now have free online math tutors. The tutors also teach English for free."

He raised his left hand and glanced at his watch, adding, "I think we're just in time. The tutors are available from two until five in the afternoon."

"So anyone can go online and ask the tutors for help?"

Mr. Ducat nodded, "That's the idea. Unfortunately, I think we've had less than five users since the program started."

"Can I give it a try?"

"Sure, you can start your shift after you work with the tutor. What do you think?"

"Sounds perfect," Eloise rested her backpack on the floor and prepared to meet with a math tutor somewhere in the online world. Her library card gave her access to the educational opportunity. Eloise wondered what other resources were free to those who asked.

The entire interaction with Mr. Ducat felt strange. Eloise had thought he was covering up murders, but his actions were kind and helpful. She wondered if he was simply trying to get her off his trail. Eloise watched as a message from the math tutor appeared in the bottom corner of the screen. She decided to focus on one thing at a time. At that moment, she had some pressing math questions.

After a productive tutoring session, Eloise finished her shift at the library without incident. She felt relieved to have addressed her nagging questions. She waved to Cali as she prepared to go home. Bookshelves towered above her as she made her way toward the door. A pool of red on a middle shelf caught

Eloise's attention. She came to an abrupt halt as she stared at the scarlet stain. Eloise's face paled as she tried to decipher what it could be. The substance looked fresh as it trailed down the top shelf and threatened to drip onto the books below.

Alerted by Eloise's sudden stop, Cali went over to see what the trouble was. With a groan, Cali darted away and returned with a napkin and a bottle of cleaning solution. She motioned to the spot. "I hate when this happens. I'm always cleaning up gross messes."

Eloise didn't know what to say as she watched Cali fuss over the seepage, and she didn't know what to think of her treating it like a common occurrence. Eloise locked her gaze on the blood-colored stain, committing it to memory. She noted the irony of it lurking next to the crime novels.

***

Eloise returned home exhilarated by her time at the library. She had earned good money, found a possible clue to the mystery in the basement, and received free help from a math tutor. Maybe her job at the haunted library wasn't so bad after all.

Eloise settled into the beanbag chair in the living room and pulled a few folders out of her backpack. She had planned to study, but as soon as her mother entered the room, her mind drifted to Dorothy's gift. Eloise needed to find some way to get her little sister a nice bike. The reviews on the $200 bikes had scared her off the idea of buying the cheaper option.

"Mom, do you want to split the cost of buying a present for Dorothy with me? I want to get her a new bike."

"Sorry. Your father and I already have some gifts planned. Have you asked your brother if he'd pitch in for a bike?"

"Mom, Warren still owes me the $25 he borrowed for his date with Astrid. That was two months ago! Would you lend me the money for the bike? I'm too young to borrow money. Besides, I went online and saw the high fees and interest rates banks charge for loans."

“Hmmm. We could consider a loan, Eloise. Give me a minute to host a financial summit in the kitchen with your father.”

Eloise offered a thumbs up as her mom went into the kitchen where her dad was washing dishes. She waited anxiously to hear her parents’ thoughts about a loan. She couldn’t hear what they were saying over the sound of running water and clinking dishes.

Between the math test, the gift quest, and the library mystery, Eloise felt like her attention was being pulled every which way. Having a little more financial flexibility would help lighten her overwhelming load. Ideally, her parents would lend her money without charging interest, but she figured her parents would want to make the loan resemble a bank loan as a life lesson. She quickly learned how right she was.

Eloise’s mom re-entered the living room, “Your father and I will consider giving you a small loan. If provided, the loan would match whatever terms you can find for a loan that an adult could take out, minus the fees.”

“Good enough. Thanks.” Eloise said. She bit her inner cheek. It would have been nice not to pay any interest. Still, she knew she was lucky to have parents who were willing to lend her money.

“Before we make our final decision, your friendly loan officers, Maryam and Murilo, would like to ask you about the five Cs of credit: capacity, capital, conditions, character, and collateral.”

Eloise readjusted her position on the beanbag, “Um, I don’t know what those are, but sure?”

Her father entered the living room, as if on cue.

“Ms. Alberty,” he said in all seriousness, “tell us about your capacity to pay back this loan. Do you have a steady income?”

Eloise loved that her parents were pretending to be bankers. She closed her notebook and decided to play along.

She cleared her throat, “Well, Mr. Banker, I have a job at the library, and I have no other debts.”

“Very good,” Maryam said.

Her mother leaned against the living room's door frame and added, “Now let's talk about the financial capital, meaning money, you are willing to commit to this venture. Are you putting some of your own money into the bike purchase?”

“Yes, Mom, I mean, Mrs. Banker. I am paying for half of the bike myself. That's $200 of my own money that's going into the purchase.”

“Thank you, Ms. Alberty,” Eloise's father chimed in.

“The conditions for the loan include the economic conditions in which you will be expected to repay the loan and the specifics of the loan itself. We're aware of the state of the economy, the unemployment rate, your income and experience, and the use you will make of the loan. What are the terms of the loan you are requesting?”

Eloise narrowed her eyes, “One second. I wrote down some information from the loans I found elsewhere.” Her parents waited while she leafed through the numbers she had collected in her notebook.

"I'm asking for a two-year loan of $200 at an annual interest rate of 18.9 percent, compounded daily, which matches the terms of some loans I found elsewhere. I would repay the $200 principal and the interest at the end of the loan," Eloise feigned confidence as she provided her proposal. She didn't have the total interest payment in her notes, but she and Bisa could calculate it later if her loan was approved.

Maryam jumped in. "You realize most loans require partial repayments each month, correct?"

Eloise straightened, "Yes, but I'm looking to make a single payment at the end of the loan, because I'll be in better financial shape then. I have a Treasury bond that matures around that time."

"I see," said Maryam, remembering one of the kind financial gifts that Eloise's grandmother had given her years ago.

"Regarding your character, do you have a credit history?"

Eloise opened and closed her mouth. She looked at both of her parents and tried to understand what credit history meant.

Her mom read the puzzled look on Eloise's face and quickly rephrased the question.

"That is, do you have a record of managing debt well? Have you shown your ability to repay loans in the past?"

"I borrowed $12 to go to the movies last month and paid it back two days later."

"That's prompt, Ms. Alberty," Murilo responded, stroking his chin. He was enjoying his acting role more than expected. Eloise tried to keep a professional face as she talked with her alleged bankers.

"One more question. Do you have any collateral you can offer? Something we can take ownership of if you don't repay your loan, to hold you accountable? The asset you are purchasing–the bike–will belong to someone else, so that can't serve as collateral in this case."

"Yes," Eloise hesitantly replied, "You can have my stuffed animal collection."
She met her parents' doubtful eyes.

Eloise cleared her throat and tried again, "My economics textbook? My basketball signed by Caitlin Clark?"

"The basketball will work as collateral," Murilo noted, concealing a smile.

Eloise's parents shared a knowing glance before turning to her.

"The loan committee has approved your loan under the conditions we have discussed. Please think it over after studying for your math test, and let us know if you choose to accept it."

Eloise appreciated the help and quickly hugged her parents. She was one step closer to financial success. If only her library mystery were so simple.

Chapter 14

Eloise found it tough to apply abstract math lessons about things like vectors, logarithms, and proofs to real life. Luckily, Mr. Schnell liked to teach using real-world examples. He was all about math, but not the type that lived on chalkboards devoid of context. Three decades of students whispering "we'll never use this" had changed his approach. He described his class as "the mathematics of life," and he explained math almost exclusively using realistic examples. Money made frequent appearances in his lectures.

That day in class, Eloise learned why people say "time is money." Mr. Schnell held up his watch and explained, "Every hour you waste costs the money you could have earned, or the fun you could have had, in that time. If you could earn $15 per hour, an hour wasted costs you $15. If you waste an hour that you could have spent canoeing, the cost of that wasted hour is the value of a canoe ride. The high cost of wasted time explains why people spend so much money on time-saving devices like dishwashers, microwave ovens, and hair dryers."

Eloise whispered to her friend, Jackie, “Can I justify buying a Mustang convertible since the time it would save me is money?”

Mr. Schnell went on to discuss three reasons having money now is better than having the same amount of money in the future. Seeing Eloise whispering, he called on her. “Miss Alberty, what is the name of this concept?”

Eloise was stumped. She replied, “I call it, why I’m willing to pay interest for a loan.”

Mr. Schnell stroked his chin. “It is why you are willing to pay interest for your loan. If you didn’t prefer to have the money now, you wouldn’t pay interest plus the borrowed amount later in exchange for that privilege. But that is not the name of the concept.”

Mr. Schnell leaned toward Jackie the way Eloise had a moment before and whispered, “It is the time value of money.”

Eloise knew the first two reasons for the time value of money from her discussions with her mother about discounting the future. One was the reason many people failed the marshmallow test: people hate to wait. They prefer to have money now so they don't have to delay gratification.

The second reason was that future events might make it harder to enjoy the money later on. Mr. Schnell explained that reason with the example of poor health. Eloise also remembered Maryam's example about the zombie apocalypse. Talk about bad health. Eloise and Maryam loved to watch zombie movies around Halloween. Murilo didn't, but he took the opportunity to eat popcorn with his family.

Mr. Schnell explained that the third reason for the time value of money was that having money now instead of later makes it possible to invest the money now and receive even more money later. He wrote "Makes investment possible" on the whiteboard and turned his gaze to the class. "For these reasons, most people discount the future at a rate that depends on their patience, outlook, and investment options."

"Think about the interest rate I'd have to pay you to borrow $100 from you today with the promise to repay you in a year. The lowest interest rate you would accept is a good indication of your discount rate for the future. At one extreme, suppose you don't care about any of the reasons I just explained. Perhaps the money will otherwise sit in a shoebox under your bed for the next year, and you're unconcerned about waiting to use the money. If you're indifferent between having $100 now or in a year, your discount rate is zero. That means you could charge me no interest and be content getting $100 back in a year. If anyone would like to give me an interest-free loan of $100, I'd be happy to put your money to work giving me interest for a year. Anyone? Anyone?"

There were no takers.

"In contrast, if you really want to use your money now, I'd have to pay a high interest rate to convince you to let me borrow that money. That means you have a high discount rate for the future." Mr. Schnell scanned the room for someone nodding their head.

"Daniel, how much interest would I have to pay you in a year for a $100 loan starting today?"

"Twenty-five dollars," Daniel called from the back of the room.

"That $25 is 25 percent of $100, so we've determined that your discount rate is 25 percent."

The bell chimed as Mr. Schnell was about to continue. He placed a cap on the black whiteboard marker and called out reluctantly, "Class dismissed."

This time, Eloise was ready. She beelined to the front of the classroom and asked, "Mr. Schnell, do you have any extra practice problems? I learn better with examples and I think they would be helpful when I speak with a tutor."

Mr. Schnell reached into a folder and handed Eloise a document. He explained, "Here are three more word problems that we haven't explored in class. I'll make more copies and hand them out to everyone as extra practice next period. You can keep this copy and get a head start."

Eloise held the paper with two hands. "Thank you, Mr. Schnell," she said gleefully as she dashed out of the classroom and made it to her next class without a minute to spare.

After school, Bisa and Eloise sequestered themselves in a library study room to practice story problems in preparation for their looming math test. Mocking the silliness of some of the problems they received, they concocted a few of their own.

“El, I’ve got one for you,” Bisa announced, “Are you ready?”

“Not really, but sure. Ready!” She tapped her pink marker on the whiteboard and playfully hopped from one leg to the other.

“Ava wins the lottery. The rules say she can receive $600,000 today or $1,000,000 in five years. She likes the idea of getting a larger amount but she also has a strong preference to have money sooner rather than later. She sees a chance of a zombie apocalypse in the next five years in which she might have her leg gnawed off and be unable to enjoy surfing vacations as much afterward. Her annual discount rate for the future is 12 percent. Should she take the $600,000 now or the million in five years?”

Eloise wrote the present value formula on the board:

$$\text{Present Value} = \text{Future Value}/(1 + \text{Discount Rate})^N$$

N is the number of years until the future value would be received.

She plugged the story's values into the formula to obtain:

$$\text{Present Value} = \$1{,}000{,}000/(1 + 0.12)^5 = \$567{,}427.$$

Stepping back to admire her work, she announced, "Solving for the present value, we find that Ava would only get $567,427 in value today from knowing she would receive $1,000,000 in five years. That value is less than the $600,000 she could receive today from an immediate payment, so she should take the $600,000 now and go surfing, baby!"

"Yes!"

"Okay, Bisa, your turn. Let's look at compound interest. Suppose Ally borrows $200 for two years at an annual interest rate of 18.9 percent compounded daily. If she doesn't make any payments until the end, and there are no penalties or other fees, how much will she owe after two years, including the principal amount she borrowed and the accumulated interest?"

"Okay, Ally," Bisa teased as she wrote out the problem.

"A name may have been changed to protect the innocent," Eloise admitted.

"Or not so innocent," Bisa countered. "With compounding C times per year, the payoff for an amount $X borrowed for N years at an annual interest rate R is found with this formula." She wrote:

$$\$X(1 + R/C)^{N \times C}$$

"Plugging in the values for X, R, C, and N, we find the payoff amount as shown here."

$$\$200(1 + 0.189/365)^{2 \times 365} = \$291.84."$$

Eloise pointed at the payoff. “Dang! That’s $91.84 in interest on top of the borrowed $200. What if Ally had a credit card? Could she put $200 on that for two years?”

“Credit card debt is an expensive way to pay for things,” Bisa advised. “If that $200 were an unpaid credit card balance, Ally would have to pay late fees and a higher interest rate for not making monthly payments.”

“I’m beginning to think borrowing money is a lot of hassle and creates a lot of expense,” Eloise despaired.

“Yeah, unless you’re buying something big, like a house, in which case most people can’t avoid borrowing. But my mom says home loans have relatively low “mortgage” interest rates because the lender has your home as collateral. If you don’t repay the loan, the lender gets the home, so it's safer than a lot of other loans for the lender.”

Eloise thought about the collateral she had offered for the proposed bike loan. She could keep the collateral by paying off the loan as promised, but the interest expense soured her on going to her parental in-house loan officers for the money. She would only accept their generous loan if she couldn't come up with the $200 on her own.

Bisa sat back down at the table and placed her chin in the center of her palm as she leaned against the tabletop. She wrinkled her nose and pressed, "Time to get serious. How are things looking at the library? I can't believe you still work there after we saw the nighttime strangeness with our own eyes."

"I like the library, and it seems safe enough during the day, but I have questions about the people who work there. At first, I thought I had everything figured out. All of my clues pointed to one theory, but now I'm not so sure about it."

"Why is that?" Bisa asked.

"Because I think I found blood on a shelf during my last shift."

"Blood!" Bisa exclaimed.

Eloise quickly raised a finger to her lips and shushed her friend. She whispered, "I think. Cali made it seem like the situation was pretty normal. Worse, Mr. Ducat was actually nice to me. The entire day felt upside down."

"What do you think it means?"

"I'm not sure, Bisa. But I'm going to find out."

Chapter 15

Three weeks after deciding to turn down the bike loan, Eloise was on the porch on an exceptionally warm day, counting the spots on a ladybug's back as it crawled on her finger. Dorothy ran up the front steps with a big smile.

"I've decided that when I turn 13, I'm going to babysit the little kids in town! Mom says I can."

"You should. I love babysitting!" Eloise shared. The ladybug crawled to the top of her finger and slowly fluttered its wings.

"Now I just need a bike so that I can get to everyone's houses. I won't be able to babysit anyone in other neighborhoods without a good way to get there."

"Yes, a bike would really make it easier, huh?"

Dorothy nodded and ran into the house. As the sun cast her tall shadow across the sidewalk, Eloise sighed and doubled down on her original gift idea. She'd buy Dorothy a nice bike one way or another. She walked to the park to get out of Dorothy's earshot before video chatting with Bisa.

"I need more ideas, Bisa! I have to buy that bike! The canvases and potted plants won't cut it."

"Well, good afternoon to you, too! Please don't tell me you're getting desperate. That can lead to very costly actions, like going to a payday lender."

Eloise waved one of her hands in the air, "No way. I don't even like the terms my parents offered. I'm sure some real lenders ask for an arm and a leg."

"You've got that right." Bisa emphasized. "Some payday lenders give you a two-week loan in advance of your payday and charge an interest rate of around 15 to 20 percent just for those two weeks. That's 390 to 520 percent every year!"

"Whoa! And no! There's got to be a better way. Help me figure this out."

"Sure, let's try to think of a safe way for you to get some cash. I think your options are kinda limited because you're still a kid. Still, let's try and figure something else out. Eloise, how about a second job?"

"I wouldn't mind that, but I don't really have any extra time. Remember, I need to play my cards right. And for now, I don't have many time cards. Help me get creative. I've heard that sometimes you get a big-dollar bonus for opening a new bank account. Maybe I can afford to buy Dorothy a bike if I open a new account!" As she spoke, Eloise flipped her phone's camera around to show Bisa a shiny, gold-colored bike locked to the park's gate. "Dorothy needs to have a nice bike like this one." Eloise spotted the likely owner playing frisbee with her friend near the center of the park. In a few months, Eloise planned to have Dorothy riding a bike like hers.

"I hate to burst your bubble, Eloise, but I think those bank deals are for people with a sizable deposit that will stay in the bank for some time." Feeling awkward about another dead end, she changed the subject. "Speaking of time, I almost forgot that prom time is coming up. Have you thought about what you want to wear? I'm still looking around for a dress that's truly my style."

"You'll look beautiful in anything, Bisa. I have no idea what I'm wearing. The good news is that my parents are helping a lot with the cost. They met at their high school prom, so they're really into the event. They are gifting me a $300 dress budget."

"Awesome! That should get you a very nice prom dress. By the way, why do you say 'gifting'? I would just say 'giving'."

Eloise laughed as she watched Bisa's eyebrows pull together on the phone screen. She replied, "I like words like that. When I go to the thrift store to buy the coolest clothes ever for super low prices, I'm thrifting, and when my parents give me money for a dress, they are gifting."

Bisa's eyebrows relaxed and her eyes lit up. "Eloise, if you see it as gifting, we'll roll with that. Also, I have a plan. You're going to love it and Dorothy is going to get a great bike!"

"Let me guess, we're holding a bake sale to fund the bike purchase?" Eloise remembered the last time they had held a bake sale. They'd eaten half of the chocolate chip cookie batter and burned the entire first batch of cookies.

“No. Hear me out,” Bisa replied. “Prom dresses are worn once. They don’t really serve much of a purpose after prom. A lucky owner might go to one or two fancy dinners where she can wear it, but that’s rare. I’m willing to bet we can find some really nice prom dresses at the thrift store, or online, for great prices.”

“Are you shifting into thrifting and re-gifting?” Eloise asked.

“I’m drifting into twisting in a dress that’s existing!”

“Twist and shout! I think I see where you’re going with this. I should thrift a prom dress.”

“Yes. That shouldn’t cost more than $100. Then you can take the $200 you saved and cover the gap in your bike budget. Will your parents be okay with that?”

“For sure,” Eloise answered enthusiastically. “They love saving money and they’ll see using part of the dress budget for Dorothy’s bike as a good cause.”

Bisa pointed her phone's camera at a bowl of ice cream on her table. She looked at Eloise and declared, "This sounds like a plan. I'm going to end the call now before this stuff melts."

"Sounds good. But I'm jealous of your treat. Ice cream after class this week?"

Bisa laughed, "You know it."

Chapter 16

Having nailed down a game plan for Dorothy's gift, Eloise turned her focus to the unexplained events in the library. She decided to ask Mr. Ducat for a closing shift so that she could snoop around with the help of a master key. Eloise badly wanted to inspect the basement and a few storage closets on the first floor.

She knew Cali preferred the closing shift because she wasn't a morning person. Still, Eloise planned to sweet-talk Mr. Ducat a bit before he made the following week's schedule. She figured a deep discussion about finances would probably win him over.

She walked immediately to his desk upon entering the library. Standing before him, she could feel sweat on her back despite not being particularly nervous. As spring approached, the warming weather made it increasingly sweaty to walk to work from school. Maybe she'd need to buy a bike for herself. Worry about one problem at a time, she thought.

"Mr. Ducat, I've been learning about borrowing and credit, but I'm still confused about credit scores. Would you mind explaining those to me?"

Mr. Ducat's lip thinned as he put down another of his crossword puzzles. He stared blankly and then his face lit up as he shifted his thought process. "Sure! A credit score is a number that lenders use to gauge how trustworthy you are when it comes to paying back loans. The range of scores is usually between 300 and 850, with good scores starting in the high 600s. A decent credit score is important if you ever want to get a loan or a credit card."

"How do I get a good score?" Eloise asked.

Mr. Ducat shared, "It comes from good behavior when you receive loans or use credit cards. It helps your score if you make payments on time, don't max out your credit cards, don't seek a lot of credit in a short period, and develop a history of repaying what you borrowed."

Eloise held her hands facing upward as if supporting a large tray. "It sounds like the puzzle of which came first, the chicken or the egg. How do I build a good credit score if I need good credit to get a credit card or loan? And how am I supposed to get a credit card if I can't receive credit until I have a good credit score?"

"Good questions. You can start by becoming an authorized user on your parents' credit card. The companies often allow that because the primary users of the card–your parents in that case–are ultimately responsible for the payments even if your inexperience with credit leads to mistakes. Being an authorized user gets your name into the system and allows you to build a credit history, which will be good if all the users of the card use it responsibly. Of course, don't go nuts with it. I recommend starting with low levels of spending. "

"That sounds doable," Eloise confirmed.

"You can also apply for a secured credit card. That means you make a deposit of a few hundred dollars with the credit card company. That deposit is initially your limit for spending with the credit card. For example, if you deposited $200, you could use the card for up to $200 worth of purchases. The company is safe that way because if you don't pay your bill, they can keep your deposit. If you do pay your bill each month, you begin to establish your credit history. The funds you deposited will generally be returned to you when you close your account, assuming you don't owe anything. A secured credit card is a good start if you want to keep your account separate from your parents' account."

"I think a secured credit card would be a good plan if I had some extra money to deposit."

The two hovered around the front desk while a few students exited the library for the day. The small number of visitors made Eloise wonder whether rumors about the library being haunted kept people away or if the resources at all libraries were similarly overlooked.

"Eloise, I also recommend looking for other credit score information and opportunities at the websites of the big credit bureaus like Equifax, TransUnion, and Experian. I'm pretty sure Experian has a program that lets you build your credit history as you pay bills for things like your cell phone."

"Great! That reminds me. I have some bills coming up, and working here is helping a lot. Is there any chance I could take one of the closing shifts next week?"

The buttered-up Mr. Ducat readjusted his glasses and hummed. His upbeat demeanor told Eloise everything she needed to know before he even responded.

"Sure, but just take one or two of those shifts. Cali likes to work at night."

Chapter 17

Eloise's palms felt sweaty as she clasped the heavy library keyring. She looked at the clock and knew she had less than 20 minutes before it was time to close the library. Cali had given her a rundown of the closing procedure. It vaguely reminded Eloise of locking a retail store for the night. The only difference? Cali said to leave the alarm off. The information struck Eloise as odd but she had promised not to turn on the security system.

If Eloise was the last person in the building, why would Cali ask her to skip the security alarm? Was Cali working with Mr. Brown's murderer? She contemplated the possibilities while she walked around the room and locked the windows. At least Cali had allowed her to do that. Eloise didn't want to make any mistakes, so she double-checked each window just to be safe. Satisfied, she walked to the front and made the standard evening announcement.

"Good evening library patrons. We will be closing in ten minutes. Please collect your belongings and move to the front with any items you wish to check out."

Eloise looked around the room and mentally envisioned crickets chirping. She hadn't found more than five people in the library while closing. Eloise watched the stragglers exit the library. After the door groaned closed behind the last patron, Eloise sprang into action. She sped to the nearest storage room door and started trying keys from her keyring. The key for the front door had a thin band of red tape pressed to the top for easy identification. The remaining jumble of metal bits in dull colors made the keyring a puzzle of patient disentanglement.

After a tense few moments, the storage room door creaked open. Cleaning supplies and stacks of paper towels lined the cramped shelves. Eloise turned on the light and carefully inspected the items. She'd read enough mystery novels to understand the illusion of normalcy. Maybe one of the shelves was a secret lever? Eloise pressed against the shelves. The cleaning supplies jostled but the walls refused to move. So much for the secret passage theory.

Distant clanging grabbed Eloise's attention. She froze and held her breath. The noise reappeared from somewhere beneath her feet.

"The basement." Eloise shut the supply closet and headed toward the place of ill repute. On the third try she found a key that opened the locked door. Distant light called from below. Eloise carefully navigated the partially illuminated stairs as she listened to the offbeat clicks. Her heart pounded in her ears as she pushed ahead. She reasoned that whatever dwelled there must not prey on lone library staff because someone closed the building every night and no one ever went missing while performing that duty. Of course, she was going beyond her call of duty by entering what Mr. Ducat treated as the forbidden zone.

Stacks of discarded books came into focus on either side of her. With intrigue dominating her better judgment, she continued down a corridor toward the room filled with sounds and light. She eased her tilted head around the doorframe to peek in. A lone figure hunched over a desk. The man held a book with no cover.

As Eloise leaned toward the doorway, the floor squeaked just loud enough for the stranger across the room to take notice. His head snapped up as two curious, time-aged orbs locked with Eloise's startled eyes.

A deep, gravelly voice rumbled, "Who are you?"

Eloise debated running back up the stairs, but curiosity got the best of her. The man looked like Santa Claus dressed in overalls for toy making, so she felt a sprinting getaway would remain an option if he tried anything.

She cleared her throat, "I'm Eloise. I work in the library. Who are you?"

"I'm Wallace." Eloise couldn't help but notice red stains on the man's hands as he continued. "I repair library books. I also help with other repair projects from time to time."

Eloise tried to wrap her head around this story. Sensing skepticism, Wallace wiped his palms on his apron and added, "Want to see?"

Wallace opened a metal cabinet to his right and revealed a collection of brushes, tape, adhesives, scissors, rubber bands, weights, and small plastic tools. A tall lower shelf held rolls of linen fabric. "With these materials, I can make an old book better than new." He motioned to a stack of books with sturdy cloth covers in handsome colors. "Those books were falling apart. Now they're ready for another lifetime of heavy readership."

"Fine. Say I believe you. Why are your fingers red?" She motioned toward the distinct blotches on his hands.

"The hazards of bookbinding. The dye isn't the easiest to remove."

"Bookbinding?"

"By trade, I'm a bookbinder. It's not a common job anymore, but it's still valuable. Bookbinders help preserve books for future readers while saving libraries like ours thousands of dollars. You see, some books are irreplaceable, and it's often a better choice to fix an aging book than to buy a completely new one. I spend most of my time working with paper, tape, thread, and paste, but dyes are sometimes needed to restore leather-bound books to their full glory. The red dye I use makes old leather look luxurious, but it makes my fingers look, well, scary."

Eloise's apprehension melted away. "What a cool project. My dad says he likes to get his shoes repaired, but it's harder and harder to find places that do that. It's so great that you're keeping these books alive."

Wallace smiled broadly as he thought about his passion. He pointed at a stack of hardcover books that had seen better days.

"We live in a world where tons of items can either be kept or thrown away. Think about our clothes, our cars, our electronics, our buildings. So many things can either be fixed or replaced. Sometimes what we already have is better than what we can replace it with."

Eloise admired the neatly shelved books with fresh covers on the left side of the room. She felt a new sense of appreciation for old books. A new puzzle formed in her mind. "Are there ways to decide when something like a book or a building is worth fixing rather than replacing?"

"A starting point is the 50-percent rule. According to this guideline, if the repair would cost less than 50 percent of the replacement cost, the item should be repaired. This is just a rule of thumb, but it's applied by the likes of the U.S. Federal Emergency Management Agency, or FEMA, as discussed in the Code of Federal Regulations. After a natural disaster, FEMA considers a building or other facility repairable if the cost of returning it to its pre-disaster condition doesn't exceed 50 percent of the cost of replacing it."

Eloise thought of the broken lawn mower in her garage and how her parents decided to get it fixed instead of buying a new one. Wallace had spent many an evening mulling over whether his time was well spent repairing things. He was gratified to be able to share his thoughts.

"The 50-percent rule is simple, but you should also consider some specifics about each situation. For example, if you didn't repair the item, could it be sold as is? If so, that lowers the replacement cost. And how would the repaired item compare with the replacement? Sometimes older products are made better than newer ones, which adds to the benefits of repairing the old one."

Eloise shared, "My grandmother still uses the first sewing machine she ever bought. She says it will outlast the ones made today because the new ones are made with less durable materials such as plastic."

"I bet she's kept her first sewing machine but her first smartphone is long gone. Some things aren't made as well as they used to be and other things, like phones, keep getting better. Like I said, it depends on the item and situation."

Eloise looked down at her favorite pair of pants. "I patch up my old jeans because I like how they fit. I think the patches make them better. They add character and sentimental value."

"Oh yes, the sentimental value of things like clothes, watches, and furniture sure can make them worth repairing. My first watch wasn't expensive, but I keep fixing it because my father gave it to me as a gift when I graduated from college. The decision to pitch or fix also depends on how convenient a repair or purchase would be and how much each option would cost."

Eloise leaned against Wallace's desk, "My mom says she won't replace her car because she knows it like an old friend. She also says it's a real hassle to buy a new one."

Wallace added, "It's also good to consider how replacement would tap into natural resources or cause pollution."

"It sounds like you're setting up a story problem. I have tons of those in my math class. What I'd do to make the decision is list all the costs of repairing the item and list all the benefits. Then I'd add up the values in each list, and make the repair if the benefits exceed the costs."

Wallace nodded approvingly. "I may not write it all down, but that type of comparison occurs in the back of my mind. A little cost-benefit analysis can lead to the best decision in all sorts of situations. The important thing is to consider every type of benefit and every type of cost. Don't neglect things like the values of missed opportunities, sentimental value, and environmental costs. It pains me to see many people neglect cost-benefit analysis altogether and simply pitch broken things out of habit."

"Not you! You're in the basement repairing books. I guess that means the benefits exceed the costs."

"Old books are special. They have a rich history, and many are irreplaceable. Add in the value of preserving artistic masterpieces and saving resources, and the benefits exceed the repair costs by far."

"I agree. But I have a question," Eloise shared. "How do you measure things like sentimental value and environmental benefits?"

"Even if you don't pay for them with dollars, you can estimate their value. To determine the sentimental value you place on something, you want to ask yourself: How much more would you be willing to pay for *that* item than for an identical item with no sentimental value? For example, how much more would you pay to have your grandfather's pocket watch instead of a similar one purchased on eBay? If you would be willing to pay up to $40 more to have your grandfather's pocket watch, the sentimental value of that watch is $40."

Wallace gestured toward the moonlit trees outside the basement window as he continued.

"As for the environment, you can ask a similar question about the most you would be willing to pay to protect the environment. There is also a lot of information available from past research on the value of natural resources and the cost of pollution. For example, with a quick online search, you can find estimates of how much carbon dioxide is emitted when making a new book, car, clothing item, or almost anything else. You can also find estimates of the social cost of carbon, which place a dollar value on carbon emissions. Environmental damage is felt over time, so you'll want to think about the value you place on future costs and benefits. Many people discount those a lot, while other people care almost as much about tomorrow as they care about today."

"Believe it or not," Eloise said, "I know exactly what you're talking about. In my math class we even learned how to determine our own discount rate for the future."

A pleased grin spread across Wallace's face. He tapped the computer resting on his desk and said proudly, "I also work as an online math tutor."

"Small world. Thank you for saving the books and for any math help you may have given me online."

Eloise paused as she contemplated her next words. After a beat she pulled out the note she found in the book Cali had brought her. She held the slip of paper out to Wallace. "Do you know about notes like this that we're finding in the library books?"

Chapter 18

Eloise held her breath as Wallace removed the note from her hand. It struck her that nothing Wallace had said explained the fate of Mr. Brown or the red mess on the bookshelf. She might be trapped alone in a room with a murderer who could easily explain to the police why he was there that evening.

She took a step back from Wallace, but his kind chuckle held no malice. Eloise watched his eyes scan the words.

Wallace lowered the note and explained, "I put notes in the books that need to be fixed to keep track of my progress. Sometimes I forget to take the notes out when I'm done."

"This message, though. Covering body parts? A perfect murder?" Eloise pressed.

"The place where a book's pages come together is called the spine. The spine of a kid's book called *Mr. Brown Can Moo! Can You?* was ready for a new cover when I came to a stopping point. The old cover didn't look too bad on the outside, and I worried I'd forget to put the new one on before moving to the next book, which was called *Our Perfect Murder*. I wrote myself this little note: COVER MR. BROWN'S SPINE BEFORE STARTING OUR PERFECT MURDER. I'm sorry that I left it in one of the books. I'm sure it caused a real scare."

Red crept along Eloise's cheeks as she stepped closer to Wallace. "That, that makes such good sense. I'm embarrassed to admit what I thought this meant. I thought all of the talk about body parts and murder had something to do with the deadly incident down here two decades ago."

Wallace sighed. "I know many people say this old library is haunted. It's old, but I would not call it haunted. I just wish more people understood that the library is filled with fascinating, free resources and not ghouls or body parts. There's not an unsolved murder in sight. Clearly my forgotten notes aren't helping the library's image problem."

"Definitely not helping," Eloise confirmed, "I also noticed a bunch of red dripping down one of the shelves."

Wallace tightened his lips. "The books shouldn't be moved until they're dry. Cali sometimes mistakenly brings up a pile of books that aren't ready."

"I still don't understand," Eloise admitted.

Wallace stepped over to his desk and picked up an old book. The thick leather cover was worn and faded. He tapped the surface and explained, "I mentioned the red dye I like to use on these leather covers. It's a great way to bring life back into the material. I put the dye on thick and it takes a while to soak in. If a wet book is placed on the shelf, the red dye from the cover will drip down and make a mess!"

A smile inched along Eloise's face. Wallace appeared to be no menace. Almost everything made sense. Looking out the window at the scene of her driving mishap, she folded her arms and asked one final pressing question, "Why do you work in the basement? There's plenty of space upstairs."

"I don't want everyone hovering over the books before they're finished. Besides, it's nice to escape the boss from time to time," he replied.

Eloise decided Wallace had a point. She found it nice to retreat to the computer room when studying because Mr. Ducat's shadow rarely darkened that room.

As her basement encounter became assuredly non-threatening, Eloise remembered it was well past time to lock up the library for the night. She now understood why Cali had asked her not to set the security system. Her gut told her that was Wallace's job. The last thing she needed was to set off the alarms the first time she locked up the library!

Eloise bantered with Wallace for a few more minutes before ascending the basement staircase, relieved and inspired. She absently rubbed her fingers along a few book spines before she headed on her way.

Chapter 19

The bike shop's heavy glass door opened easily for the young woman empowered by pride in making her first big purchase. Eloise strode past rows of bikes built for everything from casual commutes to backroad adventures. The possibilities felt endless.

Eloise was glad to have studied the options before entering the quaint shop brimming with temptations. She wanted to run to the bike that topped her list. She resisted long enough to test several bike bells. The bright, cheery sounds eased her nerves.

Gripping the handlebars of her chosen bike as tightly as the rope in a tug-of-war contest, Eloise walked to the cash register with her head held high. She felt she had done everything right. Then she saw a plastic sign on the shop's counter that mentioned bike insurance.

"Do I need this?" she asked the red-haired saleswoman.

"It's just an option. You might already be covered. Your family's home, renters, or condo insurance policy might cover your bike for theft or vandalism, up to a limit. If the bike is covered, a deductible probably applies."

"My dad mentioned something about the deductible on our car insurance. Is it like that?" Eloise asked.

The saleswoman removed a large price tag from the handlebar stem. "Basically. A deductible is the amount you will need to pay for covered expenses before the insurance kicks in."

Since that was the second time insurance had come up recently, Eloise really wanted to understand how it worked. She felt her left eye twitch as she waited for a better explanation.

The saleswoman sensed Eloise's confusion and clearly wanted to help. She gathered her thoughts as she settled onto a stool behind the counter.

"For example, if this $400 bike were stolen and the deductible were $250, you would pay the first $250 of the $400 replacement cost, and the insurance company would pay the other $150. There is also a limit on the amount the insurance company would pay. If your policy's limit is $1,000 and your loss is $1,500 more than the deductible, they would only pay $1,000."

Eloise wondered if she would ever own a bike worth that much. "If other types of insurance might cover bikes, do many people buy bike insurance?"

"There is occasional interest in it. Some people want more coverage than their existing insurance provides. The value of their bike might exceed the limit on their insurance, or they might want coverage for more situations, such as for damage caused by an accident. Other people do the math and decide to pass on the insurance."

Eloise remembered that her father had opted out of the screen-repair insurance for his tablet PC. The insurance cost $128 per year. There was a $29 co-pay for that insurance, meaning her dad would pay $29 toward the cost of each repair that was needed. Her dad told her that a co-pay was an out-of-pocket expense like a deductible, but a co-pay must be paid each time the covered service is received. In contrast, once a deductible had been paid, it didn't need to be paid again until the next year. Murilo had done a little research and found that the price of an uninsured screen repair was $150. Between the insurance cost and the co-pay, it cost $157 for insurance and a repair, so he was better off without the insurance unless multiple repairs were needed in a single year.

"I'll think about it." Eloise said.

The woman behind the counter tapped the sign. "It's just an option, but some people like it. It provides them peace of mind." Eloise thanked her again.

The saleswoman held the door open while Eloise rolled Dorothy's birthday gift outside. Eloise found herself speaking directly to the gleaming red speed machine. "Your paint looks so much better in the afternoon light!" Eloise basked in contentment that her planning, work, and research had paid off.

Having walked to the shop, Eloise decided the best way to get the bike home was to ride it. She put on Dorothy's new helmet and jumped aboard. It was tight, but just functional enough for a short ride. Testing the bell, it really did sound like her grandmother's oven timer. Eloise couldn't wait to spend a weekend celebrating her sister's birthday and enjoying tasty treats.

On the journey home, a car rolled through a stop sign and nearly collided with Eloise and her prized gift. The risky run-in forced the insurance puzzle back into her thoughts. After hiding the bike in the dark depths of her family's garage, she found her father in the kitchen. Knowing he was one to critique insurance policies, she looked around for Dorothy before tossing him a million questions.

"I don't understand insurance. Is it a good deal or not? How do you know when to get it and how does it work? Is it expensive? I didn't budget for insurance."

"Great questions. Sometimes you have to get insurance. Almost every state requires some form of car insurance. You'll need homeowners insurance to get a home loan, because the lender will have the home as collateral, and they don't want their collateral to become worthless due to a fire or other problem. Health insurance is important because it helps you to avoid paying expensive medical bills on your own when you're unexpectedly sick."

"I can see that. Dorothy's bike and I were almost launched into the next block by an impatient driver."

Her father pointed to his head with an inquisitive look.

Eloise fought the urge to grumble as she replied. "Yes, Dad, I wore the helmet I bought for Dorothy."

"The idea of insurance is to spread risks. It's very likely that sometime soon, someone will get into a car crash, someone's house will burn down, and someone will get sick, but we don't know who. If we all pitch in and pool our money to pay for the damage to the unlucky person, we all benefit from knowing we'll have help if we're the unfortunate one."

"Sounds smart!" Eloise exclaimed.

"Yes. But there are a few complications. One is that people might be less careful because they are insured, which is called the moral hazard problem," her dad explained.

"If I didn't wear a bike helmet because I knew my medical bills would be covered by insurance, would that be an example of moral hazard?"

"Yes. Most insurance policies make us pay part of the covered loss, like part of the medical bill if we're in a bike accident, to deter us from taking excessive risks."

"The bike shop mentioned a deductible for bike insurance," Eloise recalled. "Is that an example of how insurance customers share the loss?"

"It is. With deductibles and copayments, customers have some skin in the game, which gives them an incentive to play it safe."

Eloise got back to her key question: "How do you know whether to buy optional insurance?"

"That's a hard question because it depends partly on things like how you feel about taking risks and whether you can afford the risk of not having insurance. I would always look carefully at how difficult it is to collect from the insurance company if things go wrong. For example, I'm always tempted to buy trip cancellation insurance but often don't after reading the fine print. Some policies require documentation for things like medical emergencies, weather disasters, or job layoffs, and don't cover cancellation for a work obligation, a softball championship, or a pandemic. I'm less likely to buy the insurance if they only cover very rare problems. For some other insurance policies, the price is reasonable, the requirements are minimal, and the peace of mind that the coverage provides is valuable."

"Got it. Read the fine print on insurance policies," Eloise repeated.

"Yes. And remember, any insurance company that makes a profit is taking in more than it pays out, so the average insurance customer spends more on insurance than she receives for insurance claims. That means we shouldn't think of insurance like free money. The payments you receive from an insurance company are unlikely to exceed the cost of your insurance unless you're so unlucky that your covered expenses are higher than average."

"So Warren should buy insurance for phone loss because he loses his phone more than most people in school."

Eloise's perturbed younger brother was heard yelling down the hall, "It's not my fault my phone has legs!"

Her father's arched eyebrow spoke volumes about treating Warren kindly. Eloise huffed and returned to the point of their conversation.

"What if a fictional person named Sworen lost his phone a lot and, by the way, didn't bathe. Would he get more than his money's worth out of phone-loss insurance?"

Murilo rolled his eyes. "If Sworen had a loving sister who cared deeply about him despite her insatiable appetite for snide remarks, she should advise him to think seriously about that insurance. He is the type of person who could truly benefit from it."

Eloise was puzzled. "If the people who buy insurance are the ones who will almost certainly need it, how are risks spread among people who may or may not make claims? Why don't the stinky Sworens of the world sink the insurance industry?"

“They call it ‘adverse selection’ when the people most willing to buy insurance are those with above-average needs for coverage. Insurance companies try to limit that problem by collecting information about the people they cover and charging more to insure people who are more likely to make claims. Phone insurers may look at risk factors such as the customer’s history with insurance claims, the phone type, and patterns of phone-use behavior. Likewise, insurers consider your health before selling you health insurance, and they look at your driving record before selling you car insurance.”

“Okay. I see how lower prices for less risky customers could get more people on board and help insurance spread risks across people. I’m thinking it can also spread costs over time, even for a particular person, right? Like when you buy dental insurance for me, you pay the same amount for the insurance each month. When I chip a tooth, the insurance covers most of that expensive dental repair. Over our whole time being insured, we’re likely to pay in more than we get back, but thanks to the insurance, we’re not hit with the large expenses at random times.”

“Certainly. Spreading risk and spreading expenses are both valuable functions of insurance for people who aren’t so incredibly rich that they can take a large financial hit.We’re not one of those who can take a large hit: we have home and car insurance from the Green Oaks Insurance Company. Eloise, if you want to look into our type of policy to see how it might cover that bike, you’ll find information online.”

Eloise nodded and left the kitchen. She pulled out her phone and looked into her family’s homeowners insurance policy. After reading the fine print, Eloise decided not to buy the bike insurance. It turned out that the most likely problems for Dorothy, theft and vandalism, were covered by her family’s existing policy. That night, Eloise went to sleep counting the days before Dorothy’s birthday.

Chapter 20

After the math midterm, Eloise's brain was on a number crunching train going in the direction of Mr. Ducat's bankruptcy. It didn't add up. He had stable employment and rarely splurged, at least from what Eloise could tell. What went wrong? Online examples of similar public library positions mentioned that directors earned between $50,000 and $80,000 annually. That seemed like decent pay. She was stuck on the problem.

Eloise did a bit more sleuthing during her shift at work. She feared it could be her final shift at the library if she was seen as a meddling detective wannabe, but she had to ask.

"Mr. Ducat, I was curious about the financial problems you always talk about. I read that bankruptcies are often triggered by health emergencies or divorce or job loss, but you haven't experienced any of those things. What happened?"

Mr. Ducat looked at her sheepishly. "They stole me. I mean, my identity. I messed up by responding to an email scam, and the wretched internet criminals pounced."

“Goodness. You’re a victim of identity theft. How did it happen?”

“It came out of the blue. I received an email saying I needed to update the security information for my bank account. It asked me to log into my account and change my password. But it wasn’t really from my bank, and the login information I provided allowed a criminal to log in as me. Then they drained my account, taking out as much as they could each day. Once I noticed, I closed the account, but it was too late.”

“That’s awful!”

“Yeah. I let my guard down. Eloise, whenever you get an email that asks you to click on a link or provide information, beware! Check the sender’s email address and the subject line for suspicious misspellings or punctuation. You can hover over links in the email without clicking on them and see the URL where they’re trying to send you in the bottom-left corner of the window. And check the email itself for awkward phrases you wouldn’t expect from a professional business team. If you think there is a legitimate need to go to their website, rather than clicking on a link in the email, go to their website as you normally would using your web browser. And, as they say, if a deal seems too good to be true, it probably is!"

"I will definitely be extra careful. Was it the identity theft that caused your debt?"

"Yes. With my checking account pilfered, there were insufficient funds to pay the people who received my checks. The fees for those 'bounced' checks added up. That triggered more fees, and I was in a financial mess. I've filed for Chapter 7 bankruptcy, which is painful, but it will save me from an unending downward spiral."

"That's good. By the way, I'm sorry for being suspicious about the book binding in the basement."

"Yes, Wallace told me you thought a fellow named Mr. Brown would never moo, or even move, again."

Eloise offered a guilty smile and replied, "Good joke, Mr. Ducat. As an apology, I've been thinking of ways to increase foot traffic in the library. So far, I've made a few videos and set up a social media account for the library."

Now it was Mr. Ducat's turn to look sheepish. "How do you even do that?"

Eloise shrugged as she sensed a potential job promotion in the works. She hedged, "Do you think the library could use a bigger social media presence?"

Mr. Ducat's grin confirmed his agreement that it could.

***

Bisa called Eloise later that night. "Now that we know the library basement isn't filled with blood, I'm dying to hear what gossip you might have about the grump on the first floor. Did Mr. Ducat bare his soul? Where is all his money going? I'm betting on gambling losses."

Eloise paused, wondering whether Bisa would be disappointed or relieved that her theory was off. "I've got the gossip, but in truth, he's a victim of identity theft. I think he's actually a nice guy who was blindsided by evil in the financial world. He was too trusting of a fraudulent email message, and the next thing he knew his bank account was empty."

The phone line hummed as Bisa empathized, "Oh no! That's so sad. It wasn't an empty heart that made him cold to people, it was an empty bank account!" Bisa looked out her bedroom window at the schoolyard across the street, where kids played basketball in the glowing light cast from a nearby lamp post.

"Yeah, I think he's a good guy inside. So much isn't as it appears. Like Wallace's book restoration that we thought was human dismemberment! And that scary light in the library basement that was really just helping treasured books come back to life."

"That light takes a dark place and makes good things happen," Bisa observed, watching someone take a bank shot in the schoolyard.

"Maybe we all need a light like that."

Chapter 21

Dorothy stood up with tears in her eyes. Her golden birthday crown sparkled under the brass hanging lamp in the Alberty family living room.

“Mom and Dad, thank you for the great gifts. I’ll call the bugs I draw on my two new canvases Maryam and Murilo. For inspiration, I’ll watch for bugs crawling around on my seven new potted plants.”

“Eloise, thanks for the card, and for that slice of pizza a while back.”

“One more thing,” Eloise said, pointing toward the porch. “Let’s step out for a moment.” As the family assembled outside, Eloise disappeared into the garage.

Seconds later, Eloise emerged with the product of her hard work, planning, thrifting, and newfound financial wisdom. The bright smile on Dorothy’s face justified her efforts instantly. “No way! Thank you, Eloise! With that bike I will earn so much money babysitting that I’ll need to ask for your advice about index funds. I don’t really know what index funds are, but I heard you and Bisa talking about them and I can't wait to learn!"

"Sounds like a plan, Sis," Eloise confirmed, gleaming with pride.

When Dorothy rang the bell on her handlebars, her mother announced, "That reminds me: I have freshly-baked brownies." The porch filled with laughter as Maryam handed out gooey squares of chocolaty perfection. Everyone returned to the kitchen to get seconds or even thirds. Warren wiped the mixing bowl with his hand and somehow succeeded in shoving all five fingers into his mouth at once. Before the pan dwindled to a paltry handful of crumbs, Eloise wrapped a large brownie in a napkin to share with Bisa later.

With melted chocolate on their lips, the Albertys sang Happy Birthday to Dorothy. After the family watched a zombie movie, Eloise ambled into her bedroom. Her eyes rested on a book that Wallace had given her as thanks for her social media campaign to rekindle interest in the library. Wallace had let her choose from a stack of repaired books that were taken out of circulation. Her selection was a mystery novel. The vibrant purple cover and elegant cursive font had practically called her name. The fine linen cover tickled her fingers as she opened it to the first page.

Surprise filled Eloise's face and she mouthed, "The library has another mystery to solve!"

About the Authors

Camille Cabrera (she/her) is a bestselling independent author. She obtained a Bachelor of Arts in Communication Studies and minored in economics at Loyola Marymount University. She later earned a Master of Liberal Arts in Management from the Harvard University Extension School. Cabrera's novels have reached the #1 spot on Amazon charts over 35 times. She specializes in mystery and suspense. Her novels often include festive holiday themes designed to offer the reader a false sense of ease while following the culprit's trail. Cabrera's other books include *Below the Water*, *Death at Devil's Tail*, *Our Perfect Murder*, *Chronometer*, and *The First Paper Cut: An Anniversary to Die For*. Cabrera has published 12 novels and eight short stories. Her work has also appeared in publications including Harvard Medical School's student-run medical humanities publication, *In Vivo*. When not writing, Cabrera enjoys reading at the beach or drinking a cup of black coffee.

David A. Anderson is the Paul G. Blazer Professor of Business and Economics at Centre College. He received a B.A. from the University of Michigan and an M.A. and Ph.D. from Duke University. He earned a graduate certificate in innovation and entrepreneurship from the Harvard Extension School and an M.B.A. from the University of the People. He served on the National Advisory Board for the AP Business and Personal Finance Course and has participated in the AP Economics programs and leadership since 1994. His other books include *Business with Personal Finance for the AP Course*, *Survey of Economics*, *Environmental Economics and Natural Resource Management*, and *Economics for the AP Course*. His research topics include stock markets, wages, unemployment compensation, pedagogy, and the cost of crime. He loves teaching about personal finance, business, and economics, and has received awards for excellence and innovation in the classroom. He is thrilled to be part of this project to make personal finance skills more accessible because he sees financial literacy as crucial for everyone.

Questions for Practice and Discussion

(Note to teachers who have purchased a classroom set: For a limited time, we invite you to inquire about a free teacher's version of these questions that includes answers. To request this, please email a copy of your receipt for the classroom set to anton42@adelphia.net.)

Chapter 1

1. What is the purpose of creating a resume?

2. What types of gifts do Bisa and Eloise usually give their family members? Do you like their frugal strategies for gift giving? In what other ways have you seen people save money on gift giving while still giving something valued or meaningful?

3. The chapter mentions that things in short supply often have high value.
    a. What is an example of a product you value highly?
    b. What is the most you would be willing to pay for one more of that thing?

c. If you had ten times as much of that highly valued thing as you do now (assuming you have at least one already), how would that affect the largest amount you would be willing to pay for one more? Explain your answer.
d. Why might businesses advertise "limited editions" and in other ways restrict the availability of some goods or services?

4. According to Bisa, how does a card game symbolize the opportunity costs we encounter in life?

5. If you were contemplating spending a week at basket weaving camp next summer, what opportunity cost would you want to consider?

6. What are three examples of opportunity costs you face in your daily life?

Chapter 2

1. Although Eloise earns money, she doesn't have much money. Based on the analogy of two runners that represent spending and earning, Eloise resolves to have more money in her pocket by earning it faster. Using the same analogy, what is another way she could have more money in her pocket?

2. How were Eloise's parents able to afford the costly repairs needed on their car and gutters?

3. What are a few job opportunities that you can explore while also pursuing an education?

4. Suppose you were the library director and Eloise applied for a job you had posted for a library assistant who organizes and shelves books and assists patrons. When deciding whether to hire her, what skills or experiences would you look for? That is, what sorts of things would Eloise be wise to mention when discussing her past accomplishments?

Chapter 3

1. How did Bisa recommend that Eloise organize her resume? What four other things did they do to improve her resume?

2. What important information did Eloise fail to include on her resume?

3. What was the reward for passing the marshmallow test and what is an example of the way self control can pay off in everyday life?

4. Eloise mentions facing the tradeoffs of daily life. What are a few of the tradeoffs related to spending that you face in your daily life?

5. Maryam says that people discount future costs and benefits.
    a. What does that mean?
    b. Why does it happen?
    c. Is that something you do? Explain your answer.

6. Maryam gave advice about selecting a job.
    a. What considerations did she recommend?
    b. Why do you suppose there are often tradeoffs between how much you love your job and how much you are paid for a job?

Chapter 4

1. What personal finance strategy helped Eloise feel comfortable buying pizza for her sister?

2. Eloise decided to go to the pizza party. Do you agree that she made the right decision?

Chapter 5

1. Eloise became a sleuth in this chapter. Identify three sources she used to research past events.

2. Suppose you were researching a small business and the surrounding area to prepare for a job interview. Where would you go to find information on news and events in that specific town or county?

3. What evidence did Eloise have that she misses a lot when she's not paying attention? Have you had similar experiences?

Chapter 6

1. Describe Eloise's strategy for finding a better phone plan.

2. When Eloise felt overwhelmed with personal finance challenges among others, how did she center herself and bolster her self confidence? What do you do in situations like that?

3. Where did Eloise go to find information about her local bank's savings accounts? What information did she find there?

4. Do some personal finance sleuthing of your own. Find a savings account at a bank that appeals to you and report its interest rate, frequency of compounding, minimum deposit, and any fees you would have to pay to open the account.

5. How much would you need to deposit into an account with a 5% annual interest rate, compounded monthly, to have $1,000 in two years?

Chapter 7

1. What is a risk premium? Why do stocks involve a risk premium?

2. Maryam claimed that lessons about handling uncertainty about investments applied outside of the financial world as well. What advice from Maryam about investing in stocks did Eloise feel she would violate in a broader context if she accused Mr. Ducat of murder in the basement with a cleaver?

3. What is at least one example of uncertainty you face in your everyday life? How do you deal with that uncertainty?

Chapter 8

1. What is the most common type of bankruptcy and what are examples of the types of debt that it can help to eliminate?

2. What are the downsides of bankruptcy that make it a last resort?

3. Does paying rent make you the owner of something?

4. What are a few benefits associated with renting? What are a few potential drawbacks?

5. How does a bank make a profit?

Chapter 9

1. What are the benefits and drawbacks of a savings account compared to a checking account?

2. What is a benefit of direct deposit?

3. What does it mean to bounce a check? At the bank where Eloise opened her account, what are the repercussions of bouncing a check?

4. How was Eloise able to open a bank account despite being a minor?

Chapter 10

1. What is the purpose of a bond?

2. How old do you need to be before you can buy a bond?

3. What is the significance of a bond reaching maturity?

4. Why do bond prices tend to have an inverse relationship with interest rates?

5. Where can you go to purchase government bonds?

6. What are CDs? How are CDs different from stocks?

Chapter 11

1. What is a deductible on an insurance policy?

2. What did Bisa and Eloise do to narrow down the options for a car repair shop?

3. What would you do if you were in Eloise's position, not having enough money to pay for both the planned gift and the car repair?

Chapter 12

1. Explain why food is likely to provide diminishing marginal utility.

2. Suppose you are allocating your available spending money between clothing and food. What is a good strategy for choosing the amount of each item that makes the best use of your money?

Chapter 13

1. How did Eloise receive free help from a tutor?

2. What are the five Cs of credit? If you were to apply for a loan today, which Cs (other than conditions) would be your strongest and your weakest?

3. What is a credit history?

4. Do you think Maryam and Murilo handled this situation well? What would you have done differently if you were Eloise's parents?

Chapter 14

1. How did Mr. Schell explain his claim that time is money?

2. What are at least three examples of things people spend money on to save time (other than the examples in the chapter)?

3. How much interest would you have to receive in one year (in addition to getting the principal back) in exchange for providing a loan of $100 today? What does that tell you about your own personal discount rate for the future?

4. Imagine you are given a choice between two free trips: a trip to the mountains now that you would be willing to pay $150 for (it would give you $150 worth of happiness) or a trip to the beach in three years that you would be willing to pay $200 for at that time. Use the present value formula and a discount rate of 7% to determine the best choice.

Chapter 15

1. What are payday lenders?

2. What are three other ideas for getting money for the dress that Bisa and Eloise mention?

Chapter 16

1. What is a credit score?

2. How can you increase your credit score?

3. What chicken-and-egg problem related to credit scores does Eloise point out?

4. How do you get a secured credit card and why does Mr. Ducat recommend it as one solution to Eloise's chicken-and-egg problem?

Chapter 17

1. According to Wallace, why is it better to fix certain objects like books instead of getting new ones?

2. Identify and explain the "rule" Wallace suggests for deciding if it's better to fix or replace something.

3. Identify at least five considerations that Wallace suggests to assist with decisions about repairs and replacements.

4. How would you explain sentimental value? Do you own anything with sentimental value?

5. How did Wallace suggest that the sentimental value of something could be determined?

Chapter 18

1. In this chapter, Wallace talks more about his work rebinding books.
    a. What are at least three other occupations that address similar issues of preservation and resource conservation?

    b. How would you describe the trend in use of the services of these occupations?

    c. What reasons would you give for the trend in use of these services?

    d. Is there anything you think consumers may overlook when they choose not to use the services of these occupations?

2. After her discussion with Wallace, Eloise "ascended the basement staircase, relieved and inspired." What do you suppose it meant that she was "inspired"?

Chapter 19

1. Identify three types of insurance coverage other than bike insurance that are mentioned in this chapter.

2. What are two pros and two cons of insuring an item such as a bike?

3. What is the difference between a deductible and a co-pay?

4. What are at least three things you should consider when deciding about the purchase of an insurance policy?

5. What is the moral hazard problem? What is an example of a situation in which that could affect you?

Chapter 20

1. What is identity theft?

2. According to Mr. Ducat, how can you protect yourself from identity theft?

Chapter 21

1. What was the most memorable part of this story (not just the last chapter)?

2. What is at least one example of a memorable lesson about personal finance that you learned from this story?

3. What do you think the last line in the story meant?

Index of Financial Terms

Bankruptcy
A process that typically occurs when people or businesses can no longer pay back their debts. While bankruptcy might provide a way for the people or businesses declaring bankruptcy to start over, it is usually considered a last resort. The process has long-term impacts on credit scores and future borrowing capabilities.

Bonds
A loan agreement issued by corporations and government entities to raise money. Bonds typically provide a stable source of income for the investor (the person lending the money to the corporations or government entities). The face value of the bond is the sum that the issuer will repay to the investor once the bond reaches the date of maturity.

Budget
An organized plan detailing income, expenses, and other financial details. A budget helps keep track of financial information over a set amount of time. Individuals can create multiple budgets focusing on different timelines, goals, and needs.

CD
A certificate of deposit (CD) is a special type of savings account offered by establishments like banks and credit unions. CDs are usually considered a low-risk investment capable of providing higher interest rates compared to a traditional savings account. Investors typically receive a more favorable interest rate in return for placing money into a CD account for a fixed amount of time. For example, a six-month CD requires investors to agree to leave their money in the account without touching it for six months. Withdrawing money from the account before the maturity date might lead to penalties. Before opening an account, review the interest rate, the maturity date, and the frequency of interest payments.

Checking Account
A financial account at a financial institution like a bank or credit union that is designed to provide easy access to money, such as with checks, debit cards, and ATMs.

3Ds of Identity Theft
Deter, detect, and defend.

Deter:
Prevent identity theft by keeping important personal information private and offline. Avoid sharing personal details like a Social Security number or housing details. Keep information that could be potentially linked to password security questions like the name of a childhood pet or old street name private.

Detect:
Frequently review personal accounts including credit reports and credit card statements. Inspect all unfamiliar updates from financial institutions regarding account password changes or sign-ins. Check financial statements and accounts on a routine basis.

Defend:
Minimize the damage by contacting the credit bureaus and financial institutions.
Freezing credit by contacting the credit bureaus about identity theft minimizes the damages by preventing new accounts from opening.

Cs of Credit
Character, capacity, and collateral. Helps lenders determine a potential borrower's creditworthiness.

Character:
A borrower's reputation. A borrower's reputation includes details like a borrower's credit history, extent of credit history, and payment history.

Capacity:
Refers to a borrower's ability to pay back loans. Capacity takes multiple factors into consideration like a borrower's income, investments, and job.

Collateral:
The assets or financial resources a potential borrower owns that could be taken to repay the loan. Collateral usually includes savings, investments, and other assets.

Compound Interest
Interest calculated on the principal amount (the initial amount of the loan) and on any accumulated interest. The compounding effect comes from paying interest on interest.

Credit Bureau
A credit bureau (also called a credit reporting agency) is an agency that puts information about an individual's credit history together into a document called a credit report. Lenders use the information collected and provided by the credit bureau inside of the credit report to determine a potential borrower's credit worthiness. The three major credit bureaus in the United States are Equifax, Experian, and TransUnion.

Credit Scores
Represents an individual's likelihood to pay back borrowed money. The numbers usually range from 300 to 850. The higher the number, the better the credit score. Individuals can increase their credit scores by promptly paying off credit card statements and bills. A credit score is usually calculated by considering the length of an individual's credit history, how much an individual owes, an individual's payment history, credit mix, and new credit.

Diversification
Spreading out investments in order to minimize or lower risk. Diversification helps to minimize risk by spreading out investments over different sizes, sectors, and assets. It's common for

investors to help protect themselves from a potentially bad investment by diversifying and investing in a mix of assets like real estate, art, stocks, and bonds.

Human Capital
The knowledge, skills, and experience of an individual or population.

Insurance
A contract where the insurer agrees to protect the insured from specified financial losses. For example, car insurance companies agree to assist individual drivers with covered financial losses encountered in car accidents and other car-related incidents.

Mortgage
A loan used to purchase property. The borrower typically agrees to repay the lender over a set period of time with interest.

Opportunity Costs
The cost or trade-off of choosing one alternative over another. The opportunity cost of a choice is the value of the next best alternative not chosen.

Payday Loans
A short-term loan, typically with a high interest rate. These loans are usually intended to be quickly repaid and are often considered last resorts due to the small borrowing amount and high cost.

Rate of Return
A percentage that reveals the gain or loss on an investment over a set period of time.

Risk
The potential for loss or a negative financial outcome.

Savings Account
A bank account designed to hold money for future use. To incentivize individuals to keep their money in a savings account, financial institutions like banks and credit unions typically offer interest on a percentage of the account balance.

Simple Interest
Interest based on the principal (the initial loan amount) with no compounding (interest paid on interest). Simple interest is calculated by multiplying the interest rate by the principal and by the number of time periods.

Stock
Companies issue stock to raise money. Buying shares of a company's stock allows individuals to own a small piece of that company. Stock owners or stockholders typically have the ability to vote on key company decisions. Many companies distribute a portion of their profit to shareholders in the form of dividends. Stocks are a risky investment and can become worthless if the company fails.

Work-study
A financial aid program in which eligible students are employed part time while attending school to help pay college-related costs. Payments for work-study are not loans and do not need to be repaid. Students are typically given the opportunity to receive work-study jobs based on financial need.